MUSIC OF THE TWENTIETH CENTURY

by SIONED WEBB

Preface by
GERAINT LEWIS

cwmni cyhoeddi
GWYNN

Cwmni Cyhoeddi Gwynn
Hen Gapel Salem,Talysarn,
Caernarfon, Gwynedd LL54 6AB
Tel: 01286 881797
Fax: 01286 882634
www.gwynn.co.uk

Catalogue no. 8810

ISBN 0-900426-97-7

Printed by: W.O.Jones, Llangefni

CONTENTS

COMPOSERS WHO FEATURE IN THIS BOOK

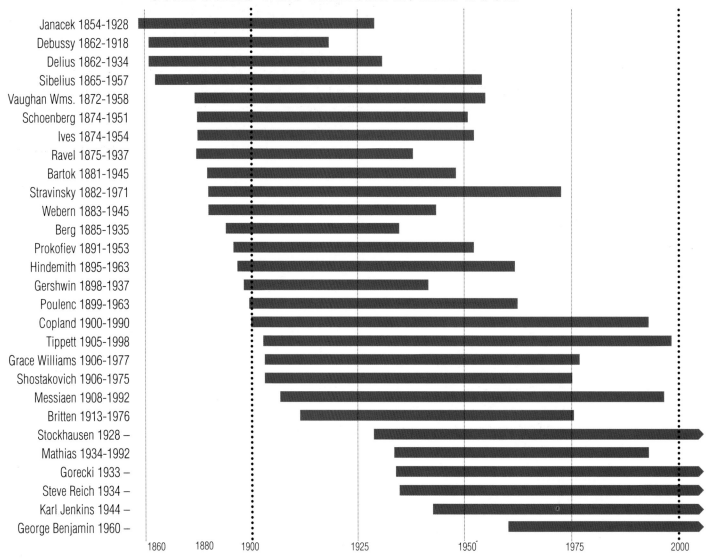

I t is with great pleasure that I introduce this new book on the Music of the Twentieth Century to the young people of Wales and beyond. This is one of the most challenging periods in the whole history of music but also one of the most exciting. Sioned Webb guides us expertly along an eventful journey tracing the principal musical paths of the century during which she examines the varied styles and idioms of the greatest composers of the time. In looking back at the history of music we refer, as if by second nature, to the music of the Medieval age, then the Renaissance and Baroque periods before moving on to Classical and Romantic music. But when we reach the twentieth century the picture becomes far more complicated. From our present perspective the general term 'modern' now seems quite inadequate to describe a whole century of dramatic and colourful developments which are so contrasted in character.

What we find therefore in this book is an attempt to earmark the main tendencies of the first half of the century - as Impressionism, Expressionism (and Serialism), Neo-classicism and Nationalism - and to define them by detailed discussion of significant works by the most important composers working in each of the four areas. Additionally, as an all-important background, the styles and composers are seen within a broader artistic and cultural context. In listening then to the examples on the associated compact-discs the process of analysis will become clear to the ear without having to leave your armchair! At the same time there are suggestions of further listening at the end of each chapter - a related work by the composer being studied and another by a composer working in the same field. Discs of these are now easily found through the various internet networks available to all. There is then a concluding section - 'Others' - which introduces works by a number of very different composers most of whom represent the second half of the century in all its richness and multi-coloured variety.

I hope that you will be excited and enchanted in equal measure as you follow Sioned on this musical adventure. As you reach its conclusion it becomes clear that there is in fact no end to the story – most of the varied paths she outlines continue into our new century without interruption. We now have every hope of discovering the treasures of the future as they appear before us. But the only way in which we can enjoy the new music of our time properly is to understand and appreciate the unprecedented developments of the twentieth century in all their glory. So make the most of the journey and enjoy it!

Geraint Lewis

Bangor

Ascension Day, 2007

PRELUDE
to the 20th Century

What we think of as 'Twentieth Century Music' doesn't begin conveniently on January 1st, 1900! But as the nineteenth century drew towards its close the grand Romantic style of the period was showing signs of major change. Some commentators can pinpoint the emergence of 'modern' music as early as Wagner's opera *Tristan und Isolde*, which was first performed in 1865. By Debussy's *Prélude à L'après Midi d'un Faune* of 1894 we are definitely moving into a new world of sound. Music up to this point was generally based on an accepted language of scales and keys stretching back to Bach and beyond. By blurring and mixing these keys and scales composers like Wagner, Debussy and others could create a new musical territory in which nothing was certain any more. And as the new century dawned these developments seemed to go hand in hand with turmoil and excitement not only in the artistic world but throughout society in general. Europe was in fact moving inexorably towards the outbreak of the First World War in August 1914. This hitherto unimaginable cataclysm literally changed the world for ever and this is perhaps where the twentieth century truly begins.

It is also difficult to define the word 'modern' in relation to music. Modern can mean new and progressive, and in looking at the first half of the twentieth century several composers stand out as pioneers: Debussy, Schoenberg, Stravinsky, Bartok and Ives are among the most notable examples. By the middle of the century there was indeed a tendency to regard these 'radical' composers as somehow more important than other less 'modern' figures: Rachmaninov, Puccini, Mahler, Elgar and Strauss to name but a few. The 'new' was better than the 'old', the revolutionary more significant than the supposedly reactionary. Such a view was perhaps a symptom of the 'avant-garde' movement of the 1950s and 60s whose thinking represented a complete break with the past, but which was also in danger of losing any connection with the wider audience which lived outside the experimental, deliberately 'modernist' ghetto.

At the start of the twenty first century the musical landscape has changed dramatically again (as this book will show) and we can now see the first half of the twentieth century from a different and fresh perspective. This is why we begin with works by Gustav Mahler and Richard Strauss (both born within two years of Debussy) which span five decades. Neither composer is thought of as a 'modern' icon and many would describe them as unashamed 'Romantics'. But seven of Mahler's ten symphonies were composed in the twentieth century and Strauss's *Four Last Songs* were first performed in 1950, a year after the composer's death. We are now, hopefully, less judgemental in the way in which we interpret musical history and can listen to all kinds of music more freely. Let us therefore hear the heritage of a remarkable century in its complete and complex glory.

Geraint Lewis

The main characteristics of Romantic Period music

- use of chromatic and extended chords (7ths, 9ths, 11ths and 13ths)
- unexpected modulations rather than to the dominant or relative minor as in previous periods
- note ranges and dynamics taken to extremes
- long, memorable melodies
- huge orchestras containing many less

familiar instruments such as the cor anglais or celesta
- a lot of descriptive or programme music depicting objects or scenes
- the emergence of 'nationalistic' music as composers from smaller countries such as Norway (Grieg) and Czechoslovakia (Smetana) felt a need to show off their own national traditions

Gustav Mahler 1860-1911 (Bohemia/Austria)

Mahler was born in Bohemia, but the family emigrated to Moravia in the Austro-Hungarian empire, and, at fifteen years of age, he was admitted to the *conservatoire* in Vienna, and then to university there. He is mainly remembered for writing developed symphonies that include solo voices and choirs and show the influence of the composer Richard Wagner. He is also renowned for his works for the voice - songs with piano or with orchestra, unlike Wagner who is rememberd for his operas.

Symphony no.7 – 2nd Movement
full orchestra

Mahler's symphonies are divided into three periods because of their different styles. The Seventh Symphony (1905) appears at the end of the second period and includes unusual instruments for orchestral music such as cowbells, tenor horn, cornet, guitar and mandolin, and it has five movements. All the 'romantic' characteristics listed opposite exist in the work - the second movement is titled *Nachtmusik* (night music), and elements of Austrian and German folk dances such as the *Ländler* appear in the third movement. The fourth includes guitar and mandolin, and all the emotion and passion of Romantic music come together in the final movement.

Characteristics of the late Romantic Period in the work

- music describing the night with the oboe imitating birdsongs in the counter-melody with the horn
- dramatic effects like muted instruments and *col legno* (playing with the wood of the bow) in the strings
- more unusual instruments like the cor anglais answering the oboe at the beginning and the bass clarinet later on
- percussion instruments like the cowbell, triangle and gong

FURTHER LISTENING:
Elgar: *Cello Concerto*
Rachmaninov: *Rhapsody on a theme of Paganini*

Richard Strauss 1864-1949 (Germany)

Richard Strauss was born in Munich, the son of an eminent French horn player who played in the Munich opera orchestra. His father was not at all keen for his son to study the latest developments in music - indeed, Wagner's operas and Liszt's symphonic poems were considered very inferior in the Strauss home. So it is ironic that it was for composing operas and symphonic poems that Richard Strauss came to public attention.

September from *Four Last Songs*
high voice and orchestra

Strauss was married to the renowned soprano Pauline de Ahna, and he wrote songs for her, following the examples of the German *lieder* composers. All his life, he preferred the soprano voice to any other. It was for this voice that he wrote the song cycle *Vier letzte Lieder* (Four Last Songs), which, amongst all his *lieder* are considered his best. The last one, 'September', was composed in 1948, when Strauss was 84 years old. The term 'Song Cycle' can be broadly used for a set or group of songs that are joined in some way or other, and many believe that this set was intended as a kind of Requiem for himself. The work was first performed in 1950 at the Royal Albert Hall, London.

More late Romantic Period characteristics in the work

- a series of unexpected chord sequences, for example, tonic followed by major submediant
- unexpected and chromatic modulations
- triadic chords, but extended as 9ths and 11ths with sharpened or flattened notes
- a large orchestra with the instruments' different colours clearly audible
- plenty of opportunity in the orchestra to create dynamic and textural swells to convey the appropriate emotion
- rich lyrics individually painted and illustrated – listen for the notes descending in pitch on the word *regen* (rain) near the opening of the piece
- long melodies, and the use of melisma to convey emotion
- dynamics used to the extremes, from *ff* to *pp*

IMPRESSIONISM
Introduction

The term Impressionism was first used in a musical context in relation to the work of Claude Debussy (1862-1918). It had been used in the art world prior to this to describe a group of artists working in the second half of the nineteenth century. The term described features in the work of artists such as Monet, Renoir, Degas, Pissarro and Sisley, artists who worked independently, but expressed themselves in a similar manner. However, Debussy never accepted the term Impressionism to describe his own work and the term cannot be applied to every one of his compositions.

In order to understand why the term was adopted by musicians, it is helpful to study the works of the above artists. They generally preferred to leave the artist's studio to study the effect of sunlight on the natural environment. This is what inspired them to paint impressions rather than what they actually saw, as can be seen in Monet's work *Impression: Sunrise*. The sun's reflection on the water, the misty towers in the background and the shimmering atmosphere are essential elements of the general impression created by the whole painting. Other works by Monet such as the *Water Lilies* sequence create a misty ambiguity, suggesting rather than stating the obvious.

The main composers who adopted this style were Claude Debussy and Maurice Ravel (1875-1937), with Frederick Delius (1862-1934) also displaying certain features.

The first major work composed by Debussy in this style was *Prélude à L'après-midi d'un Faune* (1892), inspired by a poem by the French poet Mallarmé.

'Impression: Sunrise' by Claude Monet

General Features

- parallel 7th, 9th and 11th chromatic chords
- the use of the sustaining piano pedal
- the importance of various intrumental timbres and special effects such as mutes and glissandi to enhance atmosphere
- use of the whole-tone scale or modal scales, not major/minor as was previously the norm
- a vague outline of the melody using chromaticism in an improvisatory style
- vagueness of rhythm using syncopation and hemiolas
- a particular interest, later, in the music of other countries, especially the Orient, as in *Pagode* or *Canope* (Debussy)
- a very large number of orchestral instruments playing *pp*
- transparency of texture

Composers

Tonality and musical language

Debussy

Ravel

Delius

whole tone scale

parallel chords

7th, 9th and 11th chromatic chords

Impressionism

wide use of the sustaining piano pedal

transparency of texture

large orchestra playing *pp*

interest in music from other countries

contemplative style and hazy outlines of melody

syncopation and hemiolas

vagueness of rhythm

General style

Rhythm and metre

CLAUDE DEBUSSY
1862-1918 (France)

Claude Debussy is considered one of the great innovators of modern music because he broke free from some of the fundamental components of European music. He studied in the Conservatoire in Paris and attracted public attention when he won the *Prix de Rome* for composing in 1884.

He associated with members of a group of artists, poets and playwrights who were influenced by the Impressionistic tendencies in art and who met in the home of the poet Stephane Mallarmé in Paris. A poem by Mallarmé inspired him to write one of his first orchestral pieces, the *Prélude à L'après-midi d'un Faune* in 1893 – a revolutionary work which was described by the composer Pierre Boulez as "the awakening of modern music." In the piece, a number of Debussy's Impressionistic features and tendencies are heard for the first time.

Some years after the composition of the *Prélude*, Debussy wrote two sets of preludes for the piano (1910 and 1913), in the nineteenth-century tradition of short lyrical pieces. Each one ends with a brief written phrase intended to describe what has been played.

La Cathédrale Engloutie   solo piano

In the first book of preludes, No. 10 begins with the words *Profondement calme (Dans une brune doucement sonore)* (A deep stillness in a tender mist of sound) and at the end the words *....La Cathédrale Engloutie* (The Submerged Cathedral). From the first note we hear exceptionally descriptive music. Although there are no pedal marks in the score, the pianist must use the pedal to create the appropriate misty atmosphere. The composer uses the whole range of the piano and the music is played very softly (*pp*). Debussy employs similar techniques in his orchestral works – a large number of instruments playing very quietly.

La Cathédrale de Rouen
by Claude Monet

LISTEN FOR:

- the role of the piano pedal in creating the typical smudging of sound
- open 5th chords creating a hollow yet crisp and clear sound
- homophonic, diatonic chords in contrary motion
- chromaticism and a swelling in the dynamics to increase the momentum of the piece
- transformation of theme, achieved by variation or different accompaniment
- the compact form of the piece evolving from a single idea

Despite Debussy's frequent use of chromatic and whole-tone scales in other works, this piece is diatonic, firmly anchored around the key of C major. The first chord is very widely spaced, created from open 5ths, followed by other chords ascending in pitch. The initial chord of each bar descends one note at a time in the bass to convey the depth of the sea, and creating a homophonic texture.

Piano

The echo of bells is created by open 5ths to enhance the description of the cathedral, and eventually the composer indicates that 'one should emerge eventually from the mist, little by little' (*peu a peu sortant de la brume*). The music swells gradually and the term *marqué* (marked) is written on the copy. Short motifs are heard along with the wide-ranging chords, and the music gains clarity and becomes more transparent. The tonality (e.g. B♭ and E♭ Major) becomes richer, the texture becomes more interwoven and gains momentum.

Piano

The music reaches its climax on the dynamic mark *ff* and a set of rich parallel chords can be heard above a low C pedal note, conveying the sound of a church organ with the sustained bass pedals.

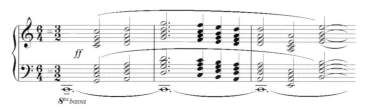

Towards the middle of the piece there is a slightly contrasting, livelier section revolving around the key of E major. A monodic line now follows the same idea by imitating the rhythm of the rich chords heard a few bars earlier. The texture here is sparse and light before swelling once again with additional parallel chromatic chords that are so characteristic of Debussy.

light texture

Piano

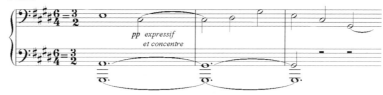

parallel cords

Piano

A quiet rumbling in the lower range of the piano gradually becomes evident while the cluster chords heard in the organ style are now merely suspended at a higher pitch. Debussy describes this device "Comme un écho de la phrase entendue précédement" (like an echo of the music heard earlier). The piece ends in this way, as if the music that previously filled the cathedral is now but a distant memory, with the opening phrase providing the final notes.

FURTHER LISTENING:
Debussy: *Feux d'artifice* (Préludes, Book 2)
Ravel: *Jeux d'eau*

IMPRESSIONISM

11

CLAUDE DEBUSSY
1862-1918 (France)

Composers in the Impressionist style were very interested in exotic and unfamiliar cultures and countries. They often composed pieces about different cultures without ever having visited those countries. Debussy shared this interest (e.g. *Pagodes* from the *Estampes* for piano which evokes Eastern music or *Canopes*, a piano prelude portraying Egyptian traditions).

One of the countries he decided to portray was Spain, despite only having been there once, for a few hours, to watch a bullfight. Indeed, many French composers of the same period looked beyond the Pyrenees for new rhythms and fresh colours – for example, Ravel's famous *Bolero* or the opera *Carmen* by Bizet. A number of the works, like *Ibéria*, are very illustrative and have a descriptive title. This kind of music is called 'programme music'.

Ibéria
full orchestra
(The Morning of a Festival Day)

Ibéria, the ancient name for Spain and Portugal, comes from a larger work called *Images for Orchestra*, which comprises three pieces in all – *Gigues, Ibéria* and *Rondes de Printemps*. Each conveys a national musical idiom: the music of England is featured in *Gigues*, Spain in *Ibéria*, and France in the *Rondes*. *Ibéria* was the first to be composed, around 1906-8. It is further divided into three pictures, conveying small scenes: a kind of small symphonic poem. In the first, *Par les rues et par les chemins* (In the streets and byways) all the comings and goings and bustle of that scene is evident. The second, *Les parfums de la nuit* (Perfumes of the night) is in a quieter style and uses the hypnotic Spanish *Habañera* dance rhythm.

The transition to the third picture *Le matin d'un jour de fête* (The morning of a festival day) includes the directions 'in the rhythm of a march heard from afar, joyful and vivacious'. This transition (or Introduction for listeners of the accompanying CD) is so subtle that it sounds like improvisation but is a complete change of atmosphere from the previous piece. The piece is so different to some of Debussy's other compositions that it gives the impression of being in a 'national' style as well as being Impressionistic, so it is an excellent piece for the study of two styles in tandem. We occasionally hear the feel of a march, with contrasting episodes of music that are very free in rhythm, thus creating a full picture of the busy morning before the festival day reaches its peak.

'Impressionistic' features

LISTEN FOR:

- the whole-tone scales heard towards the beginning of the piece in numerous instruments, but specifically from the strings, with the clarinet then replying in classical diminution

- the differences between the rhythms of the various layers, creating polyrhythms and textural ambiguity. For instance, march rhythms interrupt, or are juxtaposed with, extremely free rhythms

- the free and impromptu-style rhythms of the solo instruments, the violin, oboe and cor anglais towards the end of the piece, before the march appears for the last time in its full pomp

- the close, sometimes fuzzy texture between prominent renderings of the march

- instruments such as the celesta, glockenspiel and cymbals give the music a special colour

- strings, wind and brass make frequent use of the mute

- constant tempo changes in the 'freer' sections

FURTHER LISTENING:
Debussy: *La Mer*
Paul Dukas: *The Sorcerer's Apprentice*

Spanish features

LISTEN FOR:

- the tambourine heard at the start of the introduction and the rhythm it plays

- pizzicato from the strings which sounds like guitars (see the directions in the score for players to play the instruments under their arm)

- the strong rhythms of Spanish dances like the *flamenco* and *alegrias* which are heard throughout

- a feature of *flamenco* music or the Spanish *canto hondo* (deep song) where the music is heard circling around the same note (listen to the music of the Spanish guitarist Paco de Lucia for a tase of *flamenco*).

- instruments like the castanets and military drum add to the atmosphere

- the idea of a march on a festival day like those in Holy Week appears sporadically throughout the whole work and binds the sections together

In this piece, Debussy has managed to get under the skin of the stereotypical picture of Spain, and has created a piece filled with contrasts in mood and climate, music that is full of light and colour.

MAURICE RAVEL
1875-1937 (France)

Ravel, like Debussy, is considered one of the main composers of the Impressionist movement. He was born in the Basque country, but the family soon moved to Paris, which became the central point of the composer's life for the rest of his days. The influence of these two locations can be detected in his music – the inherent passion of the Basque country and the rich multimedia culture that existed in Paris at the turn of the century.

He received piano lessons at six years old, and when he was fourteen he was admitted as a student at the Conservatoire in Paris. He was aware of composers like Satie and Debussy, and his early compositions show the influence of both. He was interested in adventurous and advanced harmonies, and his compositions soon achieved prominence. He was also very fond of jazz music – one of the movements in his Violin Sonata is entitled *Blues*.

Asie
(from the song cycle *Shéhérazade*)

Full orchestra and voice

The arts were booming in Paris at the start of the twentieth century. Ravel belonged to a group of people, artists, poets and novelists, who met to discuss art. Among them was the poet Tristan Klingsor. Ravel was enchanted by three love poems of Klingsor's from his collection *Shéhérazade* and in 1902 he set the poems to music for soloist and orchestra.

Distant and exotic lands appealed to Ravel, as they did to many composers at this time in Paris. The Arabian mood of Klingsor's poems suited the hedonistic tendency that had already appeared in some of Ravel's music, reflecting an attraction he had felt towards the Far East since childhood.

On the other hand, he was also aware of the value of form and order in his music and liked to think of himself as a classicist. He was working on the String Quartet in F – a tribute to the French composer and his teacher Fauré – at the same time as the songs, and some of the neo-classical characteristics of the Quartet may be seen in his setting of the poems. The finished product was *Shéhérazade*, a cycle of three songs, namely *Asie* (Asia), *La Flute Enchantée* (The Magic Flute) and *L'Indifférent* (The Indifferent One).

This is the old tale from the Arabian Nights, where the Sultan's wife (Shéhérazade) is to be executed in the morning. To save her life, she starts to tell her husband stories – such entrancing stories that he decides to keep her alive so that he can hear the next episode. The three poems in the song cycle are intoxicating and tell of the riches of the Orient, its customs and characteristics, which are also reflected in the music.

LISTEN FOR:

- the silvery muted tremolando chords by the strings in the opening section, and the *pp* dynamics typical of Impressionist orchestration
- this tremolando and how it is heard often later on in the extract, creating a thick and fuzzy texture
- the oboe in the opening notes using the augmented 2nd interval typically heard in Arabian music; this motif underlies the composition's construction

- the opening notes by the singer, using the same notes in inversion
- the symmetrical hexatonic scale (D-C#-Bb-A-F#-F), prominent in the melody heard from the wind and strings along with the third declaration of the word 'Asie', which is characterised by the augmented 2nd interval

- the chromatic language, key changes and unexpected chords following each other. A D major chord is heard resolving after the above hexatonic scale
- the free rhythms in the poetry and therefore in the music, almost as if the voice were reciting the story in sentences without metre. Indeed, Ravel persuaded the poet Klingsor to recite his poems aloud to him many times as he set them to music
- the cor anglais with its rich sound, and the harmonics on the harp conveying an exotic atmosphere at the end of the singer's second phrase
- the repeated notes that the singer has in the third phrase conveying a still and lazy atmosphere (the lyrics describe a ship swaying in a harbour, hidden and alone)
- the glissandi on the harp followed by cymbals as a new section is introduced. Again, these are characteristics from the world of Impressionist music
- the triangles, Tambour de Basque (a kind of tambourine also used in North Africa) and cymbals, which add to the Eastern mood
- the alternating crescendos and diminuendos in the dynamics, conveying the passion of the words in the love songs. This passion is enhanced by the singer, in a late Romantic style
- the rubato in the metre of the music, creating a timeless atmosphere

Tambour de Basque

Asie by Tristan Klingsor

Asie, Asie, Asie.
Vieux pays merveilleux des contes de nourrice
Ou dort la fantaisie commu une imperatrice
En sa foret tout emplie de mystere
Asie, Je voudrais m'en aller avec la goelette
Qui se berce ce soir dans le port,
Mysterieuse et solitaire
Et qui deploie enfin ses voiles violettes
Comme un immense oiseau de nuit dans le ciel

Asia, Asia, Asia,
Old marvellous land from childhood tales
Where fantasy sleeps like an empress
In her forest filled with mystery.
Asia,
I want to go away with the boat
Cradled this evening in the harbour
Mysterious and solitary
Before she raises her violet sails
Like an enormous bird of the night in the golden sky.

FURTHER LISTENING:

Ravel: *Daphnis and Chloe*
Roussel: *Bacchus and Ariadne*

FREDERICK DELIUS
1862-1934 (England)

Frederick Delius is known to some as the English Impressionist, but in truth, he wrote personal music that reflected his own emotional nature. He lived a varied and interesting life. Though born in England, he spent his life mostly in foreign countries.

Delius was born in Yorkshire to parents who had moved from Germany to work in the woollen mills. He learnt to play the piano and violin at an early age, and although he worked as an apprentice in the woollen mill, he later emigrated to Florida, USA to grow oranges. There, he realised more about himself and his love for music and decided to study music in the Conservatoire in Leipzig, Germany.

In 1888, he moved to Paris, where he stayed for almost a decade. In 1897, he decided to settle near Fontainbleau in France, where he remained for the rest of his life. He also lived and worked in Norway and Germany for a period, and the composers, musical characteristics and landscapes of the above countries all influenced his music. Because he conjured images and captured the essence of the moment in his music, a number of Impressionist characteristics may be attributed to his work.

On Hearing the First Cuckoo in Spring
Chamber Orchestra

Delius's compositions were performed frequently in England during the first two decades of the twentieth century. The conductor Thomas Beecham was responsible for promoting many of them. The work *On Hearing the First Cuckoo in Spring* comes from this period (1911-12), and shows French tendencies, echoes of English and Scandinavian folk songs, a fresh pastoral atmosphere and an attempt to paint a picture of a specific moment in the music – a particular feature of Impressionistic music.

LISTEN FOR:

- the form – air with variations, as follows:

'air' or main theme

- the air being varied time after time during the work. It sounds so typical of English folk songs, but is in fact a folk song from Norway – *I Ola Dalom* (In the Ola Valley) which was used by the composer Grieg

- the diatonic harmony (in contrast to the chromaticism of a composer such as Debussy)

- a freshness of atmosphere. This is because the orchestration is slightly thinner in texture, and the wind instruments are clearly audible

- the strings as the main instruments in the instrumental canvas – this is so typical of the English composers in the twentieth century

- the way the melody changes slightly in the cadences each time, and different harmonies in the cadences, which are pleasant to the ear

- the clear sounds of the wind instruments cutting through the denser sounds of the strings

- a chamber orchestra comprising one flute, one oboe, two clarinets, bassoon, horns, and strings

Introduction: b.1-2

LISTEN FOR:

- the first chord – a major 7th chord by the strings, immediately creating a feeling of warmth as the instruments establish the mood.

- the first four notes of the air from clarinet 1 harmonised by another clarinet, the bassoons and horns. The texture sounds close and dense mainly due to the timbre of the instrumental combination. In an abrupt cadence the oboe finishes the phrase.

Air

LISTEN FOR:

- violin 1 playing the Air, while the other stringed instruments appear one by one with their harmonies to deepen the texture
- the 4ths that characterise the harmony between violins 1 and 2
- a homophonic texture, the 'Slow tempo' mark, and how the music creates a sense of time moving slowly
- the oboe and clarinet joining in, creating a cadence with a hint of false relation in the harmony (or a tierce de picardie)

FURTHER LISTENING:
Delius: *A Song of Summer*
Bax: *Tintagel*

The variations that follow

LISTEN FOR:

- the intervals in the melody changing slightly, sometimes just one grade of the scale
- the melody (air) being extended
- different harmonic treatments, becoming slightly more chromatic
- dialogues and imitations between various instruments (flute and oboe, and flute and violin) with the following motif:

- how the harmonies in the cadences change every time the Air reaches its end in its variations
- how the 'cuckoo' motif is suggested by the horns and bassoons a few bars before the clarinet plays it very quietly.

Main differences between Delius and other Impressionists

- the sound is clearer in texture
- he creates a fresh atmosphere using diatonic harmonies rather than an exotic sound with chromaticism
- his works have a more folky flavour
- his rhythms, although sounding free, stick to more conventional metres
- innocence and sincerity somehow inhabit his music, again due to the simplicity of his musical language.

EXPRESSIONISM
Introduction

One of the most influential composers of the nineteenth century was Richard Wagner (1813-1883). Part of Wagner's appeal to this day is that his music is powerful and chromatic; so chromatic, some would say, that the whole concept of key is undermined. Composers who followed Wagner made even more use of chromatic music, moving in a new direction, towards what is today known as atonal (see chapter on Schoenberg).

In this heavily Wagner-influenced world lived Arnold Schoenberg (1874-1951), born in Vienna, Austria. Although he received violin tuition at school, as far as composition was concerned he was self-taught. He was also an excellent artist who socialised with a group of German artists known as the Expressionists. In their paintings, they attempted to convey their darkest and most intense emotions, inner fears and fantastic visions, rooted in the subconscious. Occasionally, their drawings bordered on the perverse. Schoenberg and other composers attempted to convey similar emotions through music.

● Schoenberg had two students, Alban Berg (1885-1935) and Anton Webern (1883-1945). Collectively, the three were known as 'The Second Viennese School'.

● The 'First Viennese School' was the name given to composers such as Haydn, Mozart, Beethoven and Schubert, composers who had worked in Vienna in the eighteenth and nineteenth centuries

Later on, some features of Expressionism evolved into Serialism (see chapter on Webern).

General Features

• jagged and discordant melodies, with leaps and wide intervals

• dissonant harmonies and instruments played at the extremes of their range and dynamic capabilities.

• wild and irregular rhythms, to convey the most intense emotions such as hatred, love, jealousy and ecstasy

• expressionist music reflected the full colours of the orchestral instruments and could be quite subtle

• melodies beginning with one instrument and ending with another, with yet another in between; *Klangfarbenmelodie* (a melody which includes tones of different instrumental colours/timbres)

Look at the works of German artists Grosz, Nolde, Pechstein and Müeller

• artists who were influenced by the above were Munch, Kandinsky and Picasso

• look at *Vampire, Madonna, The Scream* by Munch and *Farbstudie* by Kandinsky

• look at Pointillism in the works of artists such as Seurat

Madonna by Munch

Composers

Melody and tonality

Berg

Schoenberg

Webern

serialism
(or dodecaphony)

discordant

jagged melodies with
wide intervals

Klangfarbenmelodie
– a melody consisting of different
instrumental colours

Expressionism

reflecting
the world of artists
such as Munch

expressing
deep emotions such as
love, hate and fear

wide and regular metres
and rhythms

bright
colours in the orchestration

frequent
small combinations of
instruments

instruments
played at the extreme of their
range: notes and dynamics

General style

Orchestration and rhythm

ARNOLD SCHOENBERG
1874-1951 (Austria)

Arnold Schoenberg is remembered for two things in particular: firstly as one of the first composers to embrace atonal music, and secondly for his twelve tone technique of composition (dodecaphony or serialism).

He was born in Vienna, was self taught as a composer and made a living first of all as an orchestrator. Later, he became an important music theorist and an influential teacher of composition. After being persecuted by the Nazis, he fled to Paris in 1933 and re-affirmed his Jewish faith before settling down in the USA where he spent the rest of his days and became a naturalised citizen. In fact, the two world wars were so influential in his life, that he is often quoted as saying: "Had times been 'normal' (before and after 1914) then the music of our time would have been very different."

Although Schoenberg was one of the most innovative composers of the Twentieth Century, his first compositions were in the style of the late Romantics like Mahler or Richard Strauss, two composers whose work he greatly admired. However, around the turn of the twentieth century, his music became much more discordant. There were so many key changes and discords that sometimes the listener couldn't tell what key the music was in. About 1908, Schoenberg decided at last to take a big step by abandoning keys and tonality by venturing into an atonal world. The piece *Farben* (Colours) belongs to Schoenberg's atonal period.

Farben Full Orchestra
(Five Pieces for Orchestra)

Farben is part of a whole work composed in 1909, namely the *Fünf Orchesterstücke*, Op.16 (Five Pieces for Orchestra). Up until 1908, Schoenberg's compositions included either a key signature, or harmonies that could be analysed. They were also very structured in construction and form, showing the influence of composers such as Brahms. In the *Fünf Orchesterstücke*, however, the title itself suggests something unsymphonic. The pieces are extremely descriptive, reflecting the style of Mahler, or Debussy in the way he occasionally uses a large orchestra, and yet asks the instruments to play with mutes (*mit Dämpfer*) or very quietly. He also asks the instruments to play as soloists so that the listener clearly hears the timbres or colours of the various instruments. This gives the listener the impression of chamber music, with the combination of instruments constantly changing. In this work, the orchestra is treated as a body of solo instruments.

Atonality means that the tonic of any key no longer attracts the music to it as the pivotal point. A piece may start, say, on C and finish, perhaps, on G#. An interesting point about atonality is that all notes of the chromatic scale are equivalent, and so there is no pull whatsoever towards certain notes. Some say that atonality releases the composer from the shackles of the major/minor system. Others say that the concept creates anarchy in a tonal world.

Klangfarbenmelodie: a melody whose sounds are in different colours – in instrumental timbres or the pitch of notes. This is not unique in the twentieth century. Messiaen (1908- 1992) went so far as to link different chords to specific colours. After all, the word 'chromatic' comes from the Greek word for 'coloured'.

The piece is a kind of experiment or exercise in moving from the sound of one instrument to another with great subtlety. However, Schoenberg did not accept that this was merely an exercise, as he later named the piece *A Summer Morning by a Lake*, claiming that it was based on the view of the sunlight at daybreak on the Traunsee lake in Austria. It is impossible not to notice here the striking similarity to the compositions and intentions of composers such as Debussy.

 The work opens with a tender *ppp* chord which mutates, either in orchestral timbre as the notes are transferred from instrument to instrument, or in pitch as they move in semitones.

The chord changes which run through the entire piece without any thematic development give the impression of sunlight on a sheet of water. The changes are so subtle and inconspicuous that the only impression gained is that of a change in colour quality. This technique, called *Klangfarbenmelodie*, is heard time and again in the *Fünf Orchesterstücke*. The colour of the chord depends on the choice of instrument or the notes of the chord itself.

FURTHER LISTENING:
Schoenberg: *Pierrot Lunaire*
Zemlinsky: *Lyric Symphony*

There are 4 beats in the bar and the beat is constant to help you

LISTEN FOR:

- the first chord, heard from two flutes, a clarinet, second bassoon and the viola as the bass instrument

- half a bar later the same chord sounds a little more bright from the cor anglais, muted trumpets, first bassoon, horn and solo double bass

- In bar 4, the chord changes marginally as a flute moves up a semitone

- In bars 5 and 6, two notes of the chord move a semitone again by different instruments

- The appearances of the various instruments overlap as they move, making the final effect even more nebulous and subtle

The above continues more or less without pause as a persistent ostinato background throughout the piece. Listen out later on for interruptions to this iridescent canvas, as follows:

- a small syncopated quaver motif which ripples the stillness slightly

- notes from the harp that give us the impression of the sun's rays

- another motif from clarinet and harp that describe a fish leaping in the water. It can be heard in inversion a few beats later

- an occasional tremolo from the strings

- auxiliary notes from the piccolo with harp and celesta contributing to the silvery sound

- the crescendo and diminuendo in the dynamics in the final bars so that the piece ends *ppp*

- the freedom in form and structure and strict beat

ALBAN BERG
1885-1935 (Austria)

Berg was born in Vienna, the third of four children. His father died in 1900, and Berg responded to the bereavement by starting to teach himself how to compose. Later on he was taught by Schoenberg. He was one of an elite arts group in Vienna in the early years of the new decade which included the artist Klimt and the the poet Peter Altenberg. In 1911 he married the daughter of one of the city's noblemen, which meant that he could spend all his time composing. As a young man, his interest in poetry almost surpassed his interest in music, and during his time as a student of Schoenberg he published the *Sieben frühe Lieder* (Seven Early Songs). His early interest in literature was a great advantage later in life when he came to set words in song.

From 1915 to 1918 he served in the Austrian army. It was during a period of leave in 1917 that he started writing the opera *Wozzeck*, which he finished in 1922. His first breakthrough came when parts of this opera were performed for the first time in 1924. The work was performed in its entirety in 1925. All the major European opera houses wanted to stage the opera and so Berg was able to live comfortably for the rest of his life on the royalty payments.

Wozzeck, Act III scene 1 (Marie's remorse)

`Opera`

Wozzeck is the first well-known opera to use atonality as its musical language. Berg emulated his teacher Schoenberg in this respect in order to use the freedom of atonality to convey emotions and even how the various characters in the opera were thinking. Berg fully realised how atonal music could convey the most intense emotions. Not only was atonal music perfectly suited to convey states of madness, but also strong themes such as love and hate. The one strong theme that stands out above all others in this piece is the struggle of ordinary people to retain some dignity in their lives in the face of violence. It is a successful theme due to the power of atonal music.

The main characters are Wozzeck, a soldier, and Marie, his common law wife. The Captain and the Doctor are also strong central characters . The outline of the story is that Wozzeck suffers horrible visions of his experiences in the army which make him mentally unstable. His partner Marie doesn't really care; she flirts with other soldiers and sleeps with the Major. She repents, but Wozzeck stabs her. In his fraught mental state he walks into a lake and drowns.

Many of the words are sung in a *sprechstimme* technique, using the speech voice. Another term for this is *sprechgesang* – speech-voice. The only character who sings notes in the normal fashion, as well as *sprechstimme*, is Marie.

Berg also has a number of interesting ideas, in the harmonic language and thematic material. He also moves away from conventional operatic structures such as aria, recitative and chorus. The excerpt on the CD, for example, is in the form of theme and variations.

- the tritone interval, B to F, is used to describe the tension and quarrels which take place between Wozzeck and Marie. When this tension eases, the tritone (augmented 4th) softens and becomes a perfect 4th, as in this excerpt.

- the minor 3rd interval is used as a symbol of the love between Marie and her child, especially the notes Db and Bb.

- Marie's character in the opera is represented by a military band, suggesting her sexual appeal to the soldiers.

This excerpt comes from the beginning of the Third Act where Marie (soprano voice) reads her Bible in her room with her child, feeling remorse for being unfaithful to Wozzeck. She reads how Jesus Christ forgives the sins of an unfaithful wife. In the next act, a serious quarrel will take place between Wozzeck and Marie during which she will be stabbed.

LISTEN FOR:

Melody

- the opening interval, played by the viola and which is then taken up by the violin and cello and then by the clarinet during Marie's opening notes – the perfect 4th interval

- the minor 3rd interval (see above for the significance of these two intervals)

- Marie's opening notes in the *sprechstimme* technique as she reads the Bible

(gesprochen:) "Und ist kein Be - trug in sei - nem Mun-de er - fun - den wor - den"
(parlando:) "And out of His mouth there came forth nei - ther de-ceit nor false - hood"

- notes in the 'normal' singing technique where she pleads with God on the high notes and the words 'Herr Gott'

- the texture of the orchestra expanding as Marie's torment becomes more passionate

Variation 1

- the perfect 4th returns, this time by a solo violin in a very high register, with the cello in imitation, again in a high register, both instruments using mutes.

Variation 2

- after the 'Herr Gott' at the end of Variation 1, we come to a smaller and lighter section where Marie talks to her child. The perfect 4ths have now been developed and harmonised as seen in the following excerpt.

Perfect 4ths

piccolo 3 & 4

From this point to the end it is difficult for the ear to catch exactly which variations follow, but you can listen for the following in general:

- the 4ths and minor 3rds which you can hear when Marie speaks to her child

- the atmosphere and mood which oscillates backwards and forwards in each variation as Marie's feelings become more and more confused. At times the music is more tonal and soft; at other times, discordant and atonal

- the huge orchestra, including four flutes (two doubling as piccolos), four trombones, violins tuned up half a tone, another orchestra being used on the stage including a military band, and a third (chamber) orchestra, separate from the rest

- the instruments at times (including the voices) being played at the extremes of their range and dynamics

- the jagged melodies alternating with softer melodies – a noticeable feature of Berg's music.

Sprechstimme or Sprechgesang

This strange technique was introduced by Berg's teacher, Schoenberg, in his work *Pierrot Lunaire* in 1912. It involves presenting a note which is half way between singing and speaking.

The notes in the score are marked with a small cross. The singer sings the note shown in the stave but is free to slide upwards or downwards as he or she pleases. The final effect is a curious mixture of singing and speaking which can vary from a whisper to a scream. It gives singers the scope to reflect the ordinary and the everyday, but the effect can also be unreal and cold or exceptionally expressive.

FURTHER LISTENING:
Berg: *Lulu*
Strauss: *Salome*

EXPRESSIONISM

ALBAN BERG
1885-1935 (Austria)

From 1904 onwards Berg was taught composition by Schoenberg. The first work heavily influenced by his tutor is the Piano Sonata (1908). The entire piece is based on one idea that appears at the outset, an all-important theory in Schoenberg's teachings, referred to as developing variation. This idea features prominently in the Violin Concerto.

Berg is considered a composer who was able to combine Schoenberg's twelve-note technique with a large dose of the post-Romanticism heard in the works of composers such as Mahler and Richard Strauss. Of the three members of the Second Viennese School, Berg was the one who composed the most tonal works, because he devised his twelve-note series in a special way that included elements such as traditional or conventional chords and triads within the series. The ear cannot be expected to recognise a serial technique merely by listening to a composition, but it must be noted that a strong possibility of serialism exists in any expressionist piece.

THE COMPOSER'S MAIN CHARACTERISTICS

- Berg is more tonal on the whole than Schoenberg or Webern
- he plans his row carefully to include many tonal elements
- some of his music is gentler in nature and less extreme than that of his fellow composers in the Viennese School.

Violin Concerto Solo violin & orchestra

This was the last complete work composed by Berg before his death from blood poisoning in 1935. He received a commission from the violinist Louis Krasner to write a concerto, but as he was working on his opera Lulu at the time, months went by before he started the work. He was finally inspired to start by the death of Manon Gropius, the daughter of Alma Mahler (Gustav Mahler's widow) and Walter Gropius, an architect. Manon died of polio aged eighteen. Berg dedicated his Violin Concerto to her with the words 'to the memory of an angel'. In fact, this is a requiem to Manon, in which the violin symbolises an angel, namely the girl. The work was performed a few months after Berg's death with Krasner as soloist. This is probably his best known work.

The piece is divided into two movements, each movement further divided into two sections. The first two depict the girl's life, and the last two, death and eternity. The music is very tonal in parts, although serial technique is used in the piece. Furthermore, Berg has been able to include tonal quotations from other works within the serial framework, namely a Bach chorale and a folk song from the Austrian province of Carinthia. He manages to do this by arranging his twelve-tone row as follows:

This tone row is clearly heard in its entirety when the violin enters in bar 15 of the first movement.

Pay careful attention to the order of the notes

- although this is a twelve-tone row, including all the notes of the chromatic scale, there is a strong sense of triads in the first nine notes
- the first four odd-numbered notes in the row correspond to the open strings of the violin, and these are also the four first notes of the concerto
- the Bach chorale appears in the second half of the last movement, and the last four notes in the above row are the first four notes of the chorale transposed a semitone higher and played in the violin's low range
- the first words of the chorale in the original are translated 'It is enough: Lord, if it pleases you, free me from this earthly frame'. The final section or movement, which includes the chorale, although full of grief, is full of passion and elation at the same time

The original chorale melody as used by Bach. *Es ist genüg*

Note in particular the first four notes with the sharpened fourth note of the scale.

LISTEN FOR:

- the solo violin playing the first four notes of the chorale, heard a few seconds before the entire chorale appears with alternating double stopping
- the chorale played by solo violin for six bars with beautiful countermelodies from the bassoon and viola
- the chorale transferred to a choir of wind instruments. The scoring here sounds like the change to another manual on a large church organ. This happens three times. The harmony in the wind ensemble is very tonal, with the violins in the orchestra playing snatches of countermelody
- the solo violin imitating the notes of the wind instruments after their second statement
- the solo violin's arpeggio technique interwoven with the third appearance of the chorale in the wind. The chorale's opening notes are now repeated in fragments and as an echo in the wind instuments

- the solo violin, silent for a few bars, and the four notes of the chorale heard very quietly from the cello and lower notes of the harp while an ensemble of horns plays
- a long melody from the solo violin. Snatches of the chorale are heard in it, but not necessarily in the same rhythm. The melody gradually rises in pitch, depicting the girl's soul ascending to heaven

FURTHER LISTENING:

Berg: *Chamber Concerto*
Varese: *Ionisation*

25

ANTON WEBERN
1883-1945 (Austria)

Anton Friedrich Wilhelm von Webern was born in Vienna, Austria, and is known as one of the three composers of the Second Viennese School. He was a student at the University of Vienna in 1902, and it was there that he became interested in early music. He studied mainly with the musicologist Guido Adler, writing his research thesis on the work of Heinrich Isaac, the Flemish Rennaisance composer. Webern's interest in early music would become a major influence on his composing technique in years to come.

He studied composition with Arnold Schoenberg and met Berg around the same time. His relationship with these two composers would be crucial to the future direction of his music.

His music displays great clarity of texture, and an emotional coolness which reflects his interest in early music. He was not a prolific composer - only 31 of his compositions were published in his lifetime and his work in its entirety could be included on about six CDs. But he is an important composer because it was he, more than any other composer, who fully developed the twelve note technique (dodecaphony or serialism.)

FURTHER LISTENING:
Webern: *Piano Variations*, Op.27
Boulez: *Le marteau sans maitre*

Serialism
(alternative term – dodecaphony)

This technique was originally developed by Schoenberg when he tried to impose order within atonality. His concern was that the atonal element was too vague and imprecise, so he came up with this system. It is based on a series of notes – twelve in all, including every note in the chromatic scale. It is the composer who decides on the order of the notes, and then, the series or row can be varied in several ways. The 'original' is called 'PRIME ROW', seen below in Webern's string quartet.

ORIGINAL ROW (P)

This can be varied by setting it in reverse – RETROGRADE (R)

Or in INVERSION (I) (Db is C#)

Or the INVERSION IN RETROGRADE (RI)

Or MODULATED (P1 denoting ONE semitone higher than the original)

String Quartet, op.28 – 3rd Movement

Two violins, viola and cello

This was Webern's last published work. Since he had declared a certain sympathy with the German Nazi Party, his public career as an orchestral conductor ended in 1934 when he made an 'unwise' choice of pieces to perform at a concert in Vienna. After that he was never again asked to conduct orchestral concerts there. Ironically, that meant he had more time on his hands to compose, but his income dropped substantially as a result. He composed works such as Concerto op.24 in 1934, Variations for Piano in 1936, and then the String Quartet from 1937 to 1938.

The quartet was commissioned by Elizabeth Sprague Coolidge to be performed in the Tenth Berkshire Festival (Massachusetts, USA) in 1938. In a letter to her, Webern explained that this was a very lyrical work which should be regarded in the same light as some of Beethoven's two-movement sonatas. He stated that the influence of the fugue and scherzo could be seen in the last movement.

The row has several fascinating elements:

- the first four notes in the row, if modulated, spell the name B-A-C-H (bearing in mind that H represents B natural in German) which spurs Webern on here to imitate the fugato style – the composer Bach, of course, was a master craftsman of this style

- it's very symmetrical. The four middle notes of the row are an inversion of the first four notes, and the last four notes of the row are a direct modulation of the first four notes

- the last six notes are an inversion in retrograde of the first six notes

- finally, the inversion of the row as a whole is identical to its modulated retrograde

When you listen to an Expressionist piece you must always consider the possibility that it could be serial. If you look at the tonal row, and the normal version of that row, it should not be too difficult to follow the row in the score.

LISTEN FOR:

Features of the Expressionist style:

- jagged and enormous leaps in intervals in the melody
- the wide range in dynamics, from *pp* to *f* within one bar at times   • atonality
- the pulse being varied in each bar   • notes appearing from nowhere, without any connection
- changes in tempo – much *poco rit....tempo, molto rit...tempo* can be seen and heard in the score within two bars
- a mute being placed on the instrument and then taken off, in order to create huge contrasts in timbre

features of Bach / Beethoven:

- the imitative fugal style, so typical of J.S.Bach. The fugal subject is very disjointed and fragmented, creating a combination in style of Webern and Bach. Listen specifically for four notes moving upwards, separated by wide intervals (see bottom of page) but fugal imitation may be many bars apart, and shared sometimes between two instruments.

- the scherzo style, so reminiscent of the dance movements of Beethoven's symphonies. Listen specifically for four repetitive short, staccato notes

- Violin 1 follows the row in its original form; Violin 2 follows the inverted row modulated up a minor 3rd; The viola follows the original row modulated up a diminished 5th; The cello follows the retrograde version in its original form

NEO-CLASSICISM
Introduction

At the start of the twentieth century, many composers reacted against the emotional style and rich sound that prevailed in the Romantic period and the nineteenth century, and sought new and fresh ways of composing. Others decided to go back to the past to search for inspiration. They found that a great deal of existing material was available before the Romantic period that could be used as a framework for twentieth-century composition.

Neo-classicism involves certain features from the Classical Period. 'Neo' means 'new', so the term's literal meaning is 'new classicism'. But it can have a wider meaning also. The musicians who compose in this style use styles and patterns from before the Classical Period - for example, the concerto grosso structure from the Baroque Period or an imitative device such as the fugue. Other examples from the Classical Period are the framework of the symphony, or the mood and spirit of a dance such as the minuet. There was also a tendency to use forms such as ternary, air with variations and sonata.

Listen to some of the following before proceeding to study Neo-Classical Music:

- Baroque Period:
  concerto grosso, prelude and fugue, the suite (e.g. gavotte and gigue), French overture

- Classical Period:
  minuet and trio, solo concerto, short symphony (e.g. by Haydn), sonata

But although composers writing in the neo-classical style turn to the past for inspiration and a framework, they also introduce a taste of twentieth-century music to their work. It is this combination that leads the listener to conclude that the style being listened to is Neo-classicism.

General Features

from Baroque / Classical

- devices such as alberti bass, sequence or imitation
- style devoid of much emotion
- absolute music, describing nothing in particular
- melody returning or given a treatment of variations
- clarity of solo instruments
- contrasting colours of various solo instruments

from contemporary music

- frequent key changes
- unexpected harmonies
- intentional 'wrong' notes and dissonance
- two keys heard simultaneously
- unpredictable chord sequences

also

- flavour of the past, echoing earlier composers
- clarity of texture, unlike composers such as Debussy

Examples of twentieth-century works which have origins in earlier periods:

- Prokofiev: *Classical Symphony*
- Stravinsky: *Gavotta (con due variazioni) from Pulcinella*
- Tippett: *Concerto for Double String Orchestra*
- Bartok: *Sonata For Two Pianos and Percussion*

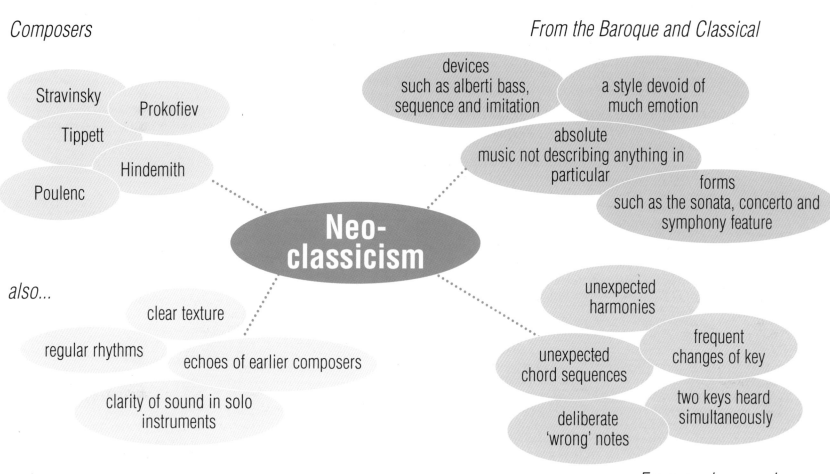

Composers

Stravinsky

Prokofiev

Tippett

Hindemith

Poulenc

also...

clear texture

regular rhythms

echoes of earlier composers

clarity of sound in solo instruments

Neo-classicism

From the Baroque and Classical

devices such as alberti bass, sequence and imitation

a style devoid of much emotion

absolute music not describing anything in particular

forms such as the sonata, concerto and symphony feature

unexpected harmonies

unexpected chord sequences

frequent changes of key

two keys heard simultaneously

deliberate 'wrong' notes

From modern music

IGOR STRAVINSKY
1882-1971 (Russia)

Stravinsky represents one of the great powers of twentieth-century music. His music has influenced numerous composers, and during his career he experimented with many different techniques and styles. Because of these frequent changes, Stravinsky is sometimes called a chameleonic composer. He lived to be 88 , and during his time as a composer he went through three, if not four, different styles.

Sinfonia and Gavotta con due variazioni from *Pulcinella*

In 1919, the ballet-master Diaghilev asked Stravinsky if he would write music for his new ballet based on the character of Pulcinella, a dashing hero of sixteenth-century Italian comedies. He also suggested that he might like to base his work on the music of Pergolesi, an Italian composer from the same period. Stravinsky agreed, and he came to love the music enormously. This was the start of the Neo-classical period in Stravinsky's career. Writing ballets was not unfamiliar to him – he had previously composed three for Diaghilev, namely *The Firebird*, *Petrushka* and the famous *Rite of Spring* which was performed in 1913 and which consisted of dissonant and primitive music. With *Pulcinella*, however, Diaghilev wanted a change.

It was not just Pergolesi's music that inspired Stravinsky to write *Pulcinella*. One of the dances, the *Gavotta con due variazioni* – (with two variations) – is based on the music of Martini (a contemporary of Pergolesi), namely the Sonata in D (1742). It is performed by a small orchestra, without clarinet or percussion, compared with the enormous orchestra of *The Rite of Spring* just seven years earlier. There is a Baroque-like tendency in the texture and orchestral treatment in the way the solo instruments stand out clearly and in the contrast between Tutti and Soli in the Sinfonia. There is also reference in the score to concertino and ripieno for the strings, which would have been the terms used for the large and small instrumental groups in the concerto grosso in the Baroque Period.

Sinfonia - Ouverture

Chamber orchestra

This is the opening piece of the work. It was traditional to have a short overture to Baroque ballets and the composer keeps to the term *Ouverture* in the opening movement. Note that Stravinsky also adheres to Baroque period orchestration here – no clarinets or percussion – and there is an echo of the French Overture with the dotted rhythms and trills. The piece contains lively syncopation and the orchestra produces a homophonic texture.

The word 'tutti' above the quotation means that all members of the orchestra play, and 'soli' refers to a soloist or group of soloists. This echoes the *ritornello* form which was so popular in the Baroque Period, and the main theme (above) may also be called a *ritornello*. Then we have solos in sequence for oboe and bassoon in the *concertante* style, as heard in the Classical Periods as well as the Baroque.

Stravinsky said of *Pulcinella* that this was his "discovery of the past, the epiphany that has given existence to my later works"

LISTEN FOR:

- imitation and dialogue between the oboe and basoon in antiphonal style
  (a more contrapuntal texture is often found in the soli parts in the Baroque)

- small countermelodies abundant in the inner parts

- the return of the ritornello (tutti) in the dominant key after the soli

- the solo section by the cello, before the music moves into the minor keys

- the colourful horn group playing the ritornello for a few bars only prior to a solo section for violin in sequential motifs, and then the return of the ritornello in the original key to close

Gavotta con due variazioni

This is a small classic. It consists of clear and bright instrumentation, scored for wind and brass only, with masterful but unfussy solos and countermelodies. The words *dolce* and *dolcissimo* in the score sum up the mood.

LISTEN FOR:

Gavotta

- the Baroque mood in the turn (~) that decorates the first phrase by the oboe

- the binary form with a perfect cadence at the end of sections A and B

- the expected functional harmony that transposes to the dominant halfway through the Gavotta and the transposition back to the tonic in the final bars

- the appoggiatura notes heard by the horns in ostinato and the sustaining notes that characterise the second half of the dance

- how the melodies and countermelodies interweave, and the way the harmony, although diatonic, starts to gather a few chromatic notes here and there

- how one instrument such as the oboe opens a phrase, and then another like the flute concludes, making the orchestration very colourful

Variation 1

- the 6/8 quavers that characterise the variation, almost giving it the feel of a slow jig

- the horn countermelody before the end of the first section, and the rather unexpected harmony

- how the variation keeps close enough to the outline of the original melody or harmony as expected

- the language becoming more and more chromatic in the second half, albeit in a very subtle and skilful way

- halfway through section B in oboe parts 1 and 2, the G and F# notes collide and accented passing notes are heard also

Variation 2

- semiquavers and even more ornaments prominent in the bassoon accompaniment

- how the melody is increasingly shared between two instruments in order to highlight their different colours, and is now five bars in length

- how the harmony becomes even more chromatic in the second half of the gavotte with the impression that 'wrong' notes are played deliberately

FURTHER LISTENING:
Stravinsky: *Symphony of Psalms*
Honegger: *Symphony No. 3, Liturgique*

PAUL HINDEMITH
1895-1963 (Germany)

For many, Paul Hindemith was the great academic among the musicians of Europe. One of the great pioneers of modernism in music, he was also a composer, conductor, educator and virtuoso viola performer.

He was born in Hanau in Germany and made an early name for himself as a violinist, establishing and playing in a number of string quartets. In the 1920s, he organized various music festivals that concentrated on playing the works of composers such as Schoenberg and Webern. During this period he married Gertrud Rottenberg, a girl with Jewish roots. From then on, he was condemned by the Nazis, who persecuted him and ridiculed his music. Nevertheless, he accepted a post as head of composition at the Berlin Music Academy in 1927 and remained there for a period until his relationship with the Nazi party broke down completely. He fled to the USA at the end of the 30s, but returned to Europe in 1953 and took a teaching post at the University in Zürich, Switzerland.

The bone of contention between him and the Nazis was that his music was too unmelodic. Goebbels, the Nazi propaganda minister, called Hindemith an 'atonal soundmaker'.

Hindemith is considered a Neo-Classical composer because he looked back to earlier forms for inspiration. His work was also given the label *Gebrauchmusik* – which literally means 'utility music', as he composed a great deal for amateurs and musicians in the community.

Sonata for Flute and Piano – 2nd Movement

solo flute & piano

Hindemith composed a sonata with piano accompaniment for almost every orchestral instrument, and most of them give the solo instrument and accompaniment equal value. This sonata (1936) comes from a period when Hindemith was composing in the Neo-Classical style. He had started composing the series he entitled *Kammermusik* in the late 1920s, imitating the Baroque concerti. Many of the elements that were evident in the Baroque Period can be seen in the works from this period, such as:

- contrapuntal or polyphonic sections, where each instrument or accompaniment has its own individual line.
- a lot of imitation in the work between the various instruments or layers
- the characteristics of the Italian and French styles, e.g. the old 'French Overture', where dotted rhythms are clearly audible
- forms that were in vogue in the Baroque period, such as binary, ternary (da capo form) and fugue.

Occasionally, too, he used a combination of Neo-Classicism and folk songs, and some of his melodies show a modal influence.

What makes Hindemith unique as a composer is the way he has used the above elements and interpreted then in his own idiosyncratic fashion. One of the main characteristics evident in his work is his use of dissonant counterpoint, where two or more melodic lines are heard to enter quite independently so that they collide against each other interval-wise, creating a series of discords. Even so, a number of his phrases include very tonal cadences.

The movement is divided into two, and falls neatly into binary form, a form that was very popular in the Baroque period.
Here is an outline of the traditional form.

A ‖: tonic → dominant :‖	B ‖: dominant → tonic :‖

The tempo mark *Sehr langsam* means 'Very slowly'.
The second movement in the classical sonata is usually slow.

Section A

LISTEN FOR:

- the flute line, which uses the Dorian mode in the opening three bars but then strays, bringing chromatic notes into the melody. Listen especially to the end of bar 2 and beginning of bar 3 where you will hear a motif (x) that will assume great importance later on.

- the piano accompaniment in two layers, the right hand and left hand with motifs that are independent of the flute. The right hand uses a series of progressions which rise note by note, characterized by a double-dotted rhythm and 4th intervals. The left hand descends note by note, creating a counterpoint in contrary motion.

- the end of the extract in the piano part, where the accompaniment can be heard using the flute's opening motif
- the flute theme developing to some extent and moving in ascending progressions
- the left hand of the piano now using the dotted rhythm previously heard in the right hand
- the section ending with a tonal F# major chord (it could be said that the music has moved to the dominant)

A short linking section is now heard. We hear imitation, or musical conversation between the piano and flute using the x motif heard in the flute's opening melody.

Section B

LISTEN FOR:

- the main flute theme, higher pitched, and playing very high notes. This theme is repeated a few bars later.
- the left hand of the piano which uses the dotted rhythm motif now in descending octaves: the 4th interval has become more prominent. The intervals, texture and dynamics of the material have been expanded – it is now in the key of D and full of massive chords.
- fragments of the flute's opening notes alternating with the x motif.
- the material that brings the movement to an end, which is very similar to section A but in another key.
- the movement closing with a tonal B major chord .

Tonality

- The music, although generally discordant, retains many of the tonal characteristics of the traditional binary form. It may be said that the work leans towards B major/minor as its tonal centre.
- It comes to rest on the dominant F# chord at the end of Section A, and then returns to the tonic, B major, by the end of the movement.

FURTHER LISTENING:

Hindemith: *Mathis der Maler (Symphony)*;
Kreneck: *Jonny spielt auf*

SERGEI PROKOFIEV
1891-1953 (Ukraine)

From a historical viewpoint, the period when composers lived under a Soviet government in the former USSR is a fascinating one. The communist government exercised an iron rule over all the arts, and strictly censored what musicians composed. None of their work would be heard in public if it was 'too difficult for the common man.' As a result, many composers lost much of their artistic freedom, and their creative urges were suppressed.

Sergei Prokofiev was born in the Ukraine, a country which was, at that time, part of the Russian Empire. At five years old he was already composing, and at thirteen he entered the Conservatoire in Moscow. For years, the Bolshevic Revolution (1917) cast its shadow over the composer. He decided to travel, and while in London he met Diaghilev, the ballet choreographer who collaborated with Stravinsky. But Diaghilev rejected Prokofiev's work, and the composer decided to return to Russia.

In 1918, his First Symphony, the *Classical Symphony*, was performed. It displayed the ideas of the past in musical forms and language, and greatly pleased the new communist government. Nevertheless, Prokofiev felt a strong urge to create more revolutionary work, and decided to leave his homeland once more in order to compose without encumbrances. This time, he remained abroad until the mid 1930s.

Symphony No. 5 – 2nd Movement

Full orchestra

In 1941 Prokofiev was in the process of writing the score for the ballet *Cinderella* when the German invasion of the USSR began. The Fifth Symphony, written in 1944, was first performed in 1945 to the sound of gunfire outside as the Soviets celebrated victory in battle. Although much of the ballet's lightness of spirit is present in the symphony, it also contains many more serious, patriotic themes.

Whilst Prokofiev's symphonies did not always follow the traditional classical pattern, to many the fact that he involved himself with the symphony as a genre makes him a Neo-Classical composer. The second movement is fast, not slow as expected, and resembles a playful scherzo. A Trio appears in the middle of the movement, so it sounds more like the conventional third movement of a symphony.

Scherzo

LISTEN FOR:

- the playful main opening theme by the clarinet which divides into two natural phrases. Although the melody is similar to Mozart in many aspects, a witty and unexpected transposition is heard in the middle and at the end. The melody is repeated by the strings.

- the accompaniment by some of the stringed instruments resembling Alberti Bass

- strong elements of percussion in the composer's use of the piano as an orchestral instrument

- the horns and trumpets repeat notes in fanfare mode to herald the ends of phrases, accompanied by a military side drum

- the first half of the melody developed and/or repeated

- the second half of the melody repeated, especially the last three notes forming the tonic triad – a feature of classicism

- various instruments play snippets of both halves of the main melody

- pizzicato on open strings

- the instrumentation getting darker in colour as it progresses, with contrapuntal figures also intensifying the texture – a bassoon is heard repeating the main theme in augmentation over heavy staccato quavers from the lower instruments

FURTHER LISTENING:
Prokofiev: *Romeo and Juliet* (suites 1 & 2)
Shostakovich: *Symphony No. 5*

Trio

LISTEN FOR:

- the cropped instrumentation in the tradition of the classical trio. Only three instruments are heard – oboe, clarinet and horns

- the oboe melody, again unexpectedly transposed to D major, and the prominence given to the flattened 7th in the melody's cadence

- the tonic chords and 7th chord on the flattened submediant as accompaniment to the above melody – this is the Neo-Classicism thumbprint on the music. (The second chord could also be seen as an extended 6th)

- the trio's main melody being repeated four bars later in inversion

- suddenly, another section in waltz form cutting in, again partly echoing the themes of both scherzo and trio in its melodies, especially the triads and unexpected modulation.

- sparkling and unconventional instrumentation here, such as piano, muted trumpets and bass clarinet, keeping up the humour with acciacaturas. (Bear in mind that certain echoes of the ballet *Cinderella*, which had just been completed before the composer started work on the symphony, can be heard)

- the full orchestra playing an augmentation of the waltz theme with the horns clearly audible

- the extract ending with a repetition of the first trio theme. The scherzo theme returns shortly.

FRANCIS POULENC
1899-1963 (France)

The music of Francis Poulenc is so individualistic that it is difficult to discern specific influences. However, the influence of Schubert and Mozart can be detected in his melodies, he uses structure and form that evoke classicists such as Haydn and Beethoven, and he wrote songs in the French *mélodie* method which emulate the composer Fauré. He taught himself to compose, and first found fame at just eighteen years old.

Like other contemporary composers, he was aware of Stravinsky and Satie, and many of his musical ideas are very similar to theirs. Poulenc belonged to a group of musicians in the 1920s who were called *Les Six* – six composers who rejected the romantic ideas of the nineteenth century, and who rebelled against the Impressionistic ideas of composers such as Debussy and Ravel. *Les Six* liked the term 'music realism', that is, music that reflected society around them exactly as it was. Poulenc in particular was an enthusiastic fan of vaudeville music, and artists like Maurice Chevalier, a star of early Hollywood musicals. All these characteristics are evident in his work, and yet he discovered his own particular style.

Concerto for Two Pianos – 2nd Movement

Two solo pianos and Orchestra

All Poulenc's concerti are important twentieth-century milestones, because he went back to Baroque ideas for inspiration, as well as composing wonderful melodies. The Concerto for Two Pianos (1932) shows obvious Neo-Classical influences in its structure and melodies, yet it is not classicism in the sense of Brahms or Beethoven, where small motifs are central to the work and are constantly developed. Here, instead, we have one beautiful melody after another. In a letter to his friend Paul Collaer, Poulenc referred to the "majesty, energy and ferocity" of the work. That, in his opinion, was what made it so popular with audiences. In this concerto we can hear a number of various devices such as ostinati, the toccata style and gamelan music, with both pianos used in the drumming style of percussion instruments. At the same time, wonderful melodies evoke composers like Mozart or Saint-Saëns at their best. The second movement opens gently and tenderly.

LISTEN FOR:

Section A

- the Mozartian opening melody. It is in phrases of eight bars, with the second piano joining in the second phrase, yet it includes some touches that Mozart would probably never have included. The chromaticism of the first two bars suggests as much, as do the bars heard after the end of the following extract.

- the same theme and how it is transposed to the subdominant after chromatic runs, and not to the dominant as in classical tradition. Listen specifically for the descending suspensions in sequence from the strings when the orchestra comes in

- the orchestration and how it reflects the classic collection of instruments typical of the eighteenth century, except for touches from the cor anglais and piccolo to add special colour

Section B

- a new quicker section characterised by dotted rhythms in the melody, which is now in A flat

- a number of chromatic modulations in ascending sequences until we reach a dominant pedal note (F) in the movement's opening key, B flat, for several bars, as the two pianos play phrases which recall the cadenza of the classical concerti

Section A

- the return of the original melody in the original key, but only for four bars this time. This abbreviation of the Da Capo is a prominent feature of Poulenc's concerti

- the suspensions appearing again, with a few differences in the two pianos' arpeggio figures. There is also some imitation between the two pianos

- a few bars before the end that are unfamiliar in feel and content as one piano plays discordant notes in 2nd intervals, reflecting the composer's eccentric nature. (The idea, incidentally, comes from the first movement)

- the typical tonic, dominant and subdominant chords, prominent in the closing bars

- how the movement ends on the tonic major 7th chord

Features of Neo-Classicism

- the movement is in ABA form but with small changes

- echoes of composers such as Mozart are apparent in the melody and harmony, but with unexpected little touches

- the tonic as a key is strong, but modulates to unexpected keys

- unfamiliar and unexpected touches in music that otherwise sounds familiar

FURTHER LISTENING:
Poulenc: *Organ Concerto*
Respighi: Suite – *The Birds*

MICHAEL TIPPETT
1905-1998 (England)

Michael Tippett was born in London. He had little contact with music during his childhood, and didn't get the support that he needed from his school to become a musician. His parents therefore agreed to support his entry into the Royal College of Music in London in 1923. He wasn't at all happy with his first musical efforts, and in 1933 he decided to return to the College to study under R.O. Morris – an expert on counterpoint, specifically sixteenth century counterpoint. This was a turning point in his life. As a musician, Tippett matured in his late twenties: it was at this time that the first fruits of his labour in its new form appeared.

Tippett had a keen interest in his environment, his fellow-man and his country. In 1943, during World War Two, he was imprisoned for refusing to join the British armed forces, and many of his works reflect his conviction as a pacifist (e.g. the oratorio *A Child of Our Time*).

Despite his frequent opposition to the British establishment, he was awarded a knighthood in 1966. He is considered pre-eminent among the new generation of English composers of the twentieth century.

Concerto for Double String Orchestra – 3rd Movement

Double string orchestra

The Concerto for Double String Orchestra was composed in 1938, and contains many contrapuntal features. Because Tippett chose this particular orchestration for the concerto, the two orchestras have an opportunity to play their own melodies, thus creating great conflict and tension.

Tippett was also a great admirer of Beethoven, and tried to emulate his ideas, especially his approach to framework, form and structure. In the Concerto for Double String Orchestra, the two fast movements, 1 and 3, follow the framework of sonata form quite closely, while the slow movement deliberately emulates the form of the slow movement of Beethoven's String Quartet op. 95.

Influences from the world of jazz are also evident. The way the principal themes soar up and down the range in improvisatory style, the unexpected syncopation between 3/4 and 6/8, and the harmony itself at times display the instrumental and vocal features of artists such as Louis Armstrong and Bessie Smith. As a result, Tippett's music is extremely energetic, while blues harmonies add feelings of deep yearning.

Tippett was also interested in folk music. In the Concerto, note the pentatonic melodies, the Mixolydian mode (G-G) and quotations from the occasional song: a pipe tune from Northumbria, for example, can be heard closing the Concerto with gusto.

Two main features should be looked for when considering Neo-Classicism as a style:
1. The form of the piece should be examined first to consider whether it fits neatly into one of the structures used in the past. Here, we see that sonata form has been used. (Listen carefully to the CD for the different sections indicated by the quotations).

Sonata form

Exposition		Development	Recapitulation	
1st subject	2nd subjects	of both subjects	1st subject	2nd subjects
tonic → dominant		modulation	tonic → tonic	

2. Secondly, look out for devices such as inversion, augmentation and diminution, antiphony, fugal expositions and sequences that reflect Neo-Classicism at its best. These are heard here also.

LISTEN FOR:

Exposition

This is the principal theme of the work which opens the movement. Note that the **first subject** divides into three, and resembles a first subject **group** rather than one theme only. The three motifs are also shared between the two orchestras

- the **bridge passage**, important because it contains a theme that derives from the concerto's opening auxiliary notes in the first movement

- the **second subject**, heard from the cello after a transposition to another key (though not the dominant as expected). The melody is less busy, which again follows the tendencies of the Classicists. It is repeated an octave higher by the violin

Development Section

The opening music returning in another key. The intervals are extended this time and we hear an inversion of the second half of motif 3. Note the difference between the Exposition and Development in this motif.

- the **second subject**, extended and changed and treated in various different ways

Examples of sequences, canon, stretto, and antiphony can be heard in the following bars

Recapitulation

The first and second subjects returing in similar form to the Exposition.

- towards the end, however, Tippett has included a Coda that brings together all the features and elements contained in the work in a very special way. A Northumbrian folk tune in 2/4 time is played by one orchestra, juxtaposed against 6/8 rhythms in the second orchestra. Note the syncopation in the 'scotch snap' in the folk tune

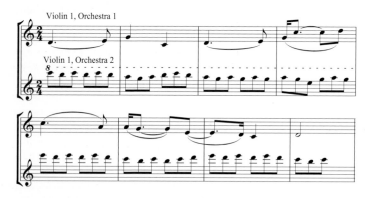

These two rhythms, one so typical of the material already heard and the other from the world of folk music, bring the work to a climax of competitive tension, but also somehow convey a feeling of great release. It is a fitting end to a work that remains remarkably popular.

FURTHER LISTENING:
Tippett: *Triple Concerto*
Lutoslawski: *Concerto for Orchestra*

NEO-CLASSICISM

39

NATIONALISM
Introduction

In the twentieth century, a number of composers became very interested in promoting their country's native music. This was not a new trend: many composers of the previous century like Smetana (1824-1884) and Grieg (1843-1907) had reacted to the fact that a great proportion of classical music was centred around Germany and Italy. The smaller countries were also keen to assert their identity.

In a century which saw two world wars and numerous smaller wars, it is not surprising that a number of composers took an interest in safeguarding and promoting their distinct heritage and culture. Indeed, in the first half of the century promoting nationalism in music was something which governments frequently did for political propaganda purposes. An interest in folk tunes became fashionable and a starting point for many composers, whether for propaganda purposes or otherwise.

As the roots of twentieth-century 'national' music lie in the preceding century, it does not always appear as innovative as other developments in music during the same period. On the other hand, some composers used folk music as a field of study and research, yielding brand new material. Composers such as Bela Bartok (1881-1945) did not just incorporate folk music in his work, but used its tendencies, features and character to create a new genre of music which is amongst the most revolutionary and inventive of the twentieth century.

NATIONALISM IN MUSIC

- features of their country's native dances, rhythms of the native language, folk songs and folklore
- the country's folk instruments or an attempt to imitate them using similar, more classical, instruments
- native scenery and landscape used as a canvas for music
- the nation's proud spirit highlighted in music full of pomp
- traditional customs or particular religious festivals depicted

GENERAL FEATURES

- the influence of modes, not only the familiar modes but also modes very strange to the western ear
- the influence of the traditional pentatonic scale and more unfamiliar pentatonic scales
- strong and powerful rhythms in energetic music reflecting folk dances
- features seen in folk instruments such as open 4ths and 5ths derived from bagpipe drones
- a more imprecise bar line and freer rhythms in less energetic music
- plenty of ostinati, pedal notes and drones in rhythms and melodies

COMPOSERS WHO USED SOME OF THE ABOVE IDEAS

Béla Bartók (Hungary)

Leŏs Janacek (Czechoslovakia)

Jean Sibelius (Finland)

Zoltan Kodaly (Hungary)

Aaron Copland (USA)

Ralph Vaughan Williams (England)

Benjamin Britten (England)

Joaquin Rodrigo (Spain)

Michael Tippett (England)

Grace Williams (Wales)

George Gershwin (USA)

William Mathias (Wales)

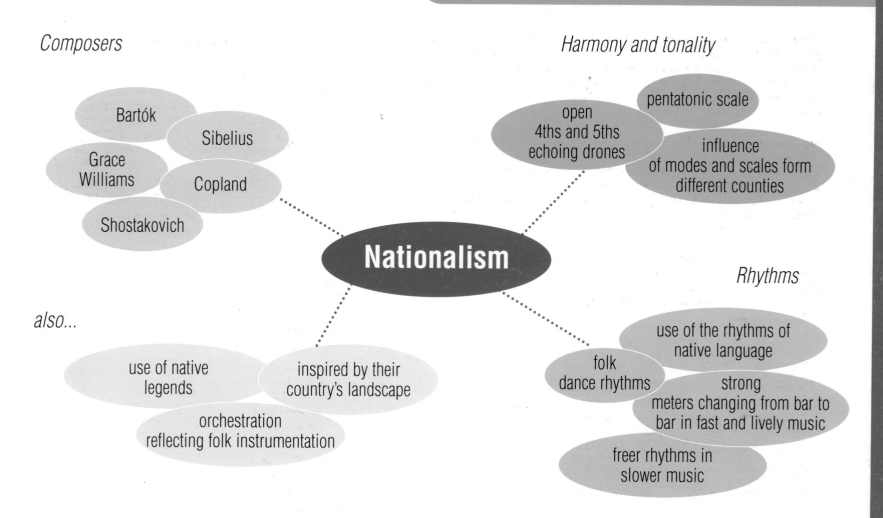

Composers

- Bartók
- Sibelius
- Grace Williams
- Copland
- Shostakovich

Nationalism

Harmony and tonality

- open 4ths and 5ths echoing drones
- pentatonic scale
- influence of modes and scales form different counties

Rhythms

- use of the rhythms of native language
- folk dance rhythms
- strong meters changing from bar to bar in fast and lively music
- freer rhythms in slower music

also...

- use of native legends
- inspired by their country's landscape
- orchestration reflecting folk instrumentation

JEAN SIBELIUS
1865-1957 (Finland)

Jean Sibelius is the only composer from Finland to be internationally recognised. He was born in Tavastheus or Hämeenlinna, a province north of the capital Helsinki, and the vast landscape of the country seems to be reflected in his music. Indeed, this is what inspired him to become a composer in his youth and to challenge his father, who wanted him to become a doctor. Though he never used a single folk tune in his work, many melodies in his early works are similar to folk songs. He is considered as a nationalistic composer because of the patriotic feelings his work engendered in the Finnish people.

Although Sibelius was born into a Swedish-speaking family, his parents decided to send him to a Finnish-medium school. Like many parents at the time, they were part of the nationalist movement, Fennoman, which aimed to restore Finnish values to a country that had been under Russian occupation. The nation gained its independence in 1917, by which time Sibelius had been honoured with an annual payment from the government to enable him to compose on a full-time basis.

It may be said that Sibelius followed nineteenth-century musical patterns and language, but his work also has a certain fresh quality which makes him an individualistic figure in the twentieth century. He deliberately avoided experimentation and the recognized schools.

Symphony no. 5 in E flat – Finale

Allegro molto – Un pochettino largamente.

Full orchestra

Sibelius composed a number of works that reflect the independent spirit of Finland through patriotic themes, such as the famous *Finlandia*, and a number of works based on the Kalevala, a Finnish epic.

He also composed seven symphonies (and famously destroyed the Eighth). Form and structure of the preceding periods were extremely important to him, but the main characteristic of his symphonies is their organic growth, in that whole movements derive from one thematic idea, or one "musical cell" as Sibelius himself refers to it.

The Fifth Symphony was composed between 1914 and 1919, originally to celebrate the composer's 50th birthday. During these turbulent First World War years, this work could easily have been dark and melancholy. Not so. The work contains a certain tranquillity and ends on a positive and almost defiant note.

Sibelius's love of nature and the countryside around him has very often given his work another dimension. This, more than anything else, is what makes him a nationalistic composer in many people's minds. The symphony went through numerous drafts, and Sibelius became discouraged at times. However, one morning, as the composer was walking through the countryside, he saw sixteen wild swans fly above, a sight that took his breath away and inspired him to write the finale to his symphony.

"One of my greatest experiences! My God what beauty! …The swan-call is close to the sound of the trumpet….A low refrain reminiscent of a small child crying. Nature's Mysticism and Life's Angst! The Fifth Symphony's finale-theme: Legato in the trumpets!"

The story doesn't end there. According to Sibelius, after he completed the very last draft of the finale, twelve white swans flew over the house, settled on the lake, and then circled three times overhead before flying away.

The composer died in September 1957, on the same evening that the Finnish National Orchestra were performing the symphony not far away in Helsinki.

The two extracts come from the finale, one from the start of the movement and the other at the end.

- Listen generally for the thematic link from one extract to the other which shows Sibelius's art as a composer and his technique in developing the theme from one idea.

- Listen also for elements of sonata and rondo forms – two great themes appearing separately but combining at the end of the movement.

Extract 1

LISTEN FOR:

- the note from the timpani (Bb), which acts as a dominant pedal, and the dominant chord suggested by the horns

- the tonic and dominant notes (Eb and Bb) played by the lower strings before the appearance of the main theme; these are also the first notes of that theme

- the great theme (1) from the horns (the theme inspired by the swans). Listen specifically for the leaps of 5ths, 6ths and 7ths in the melody and for the 3rds between the horns

- after two renderings of the above theme, another theme (2) from the wind, that has been described as a simple hymn, and a theme that creates a countermelody to the horns' theme. It is much more confined in range, and turns around just four or five notes, possibly suggesting folk influences

- the modulation to C major, a climax referred to as one of the most passionate in music

- the trombones joining the horns to add to the passion

- the theme from the woodwinds above continuing and increasingly interweaving with the theme from the brass

- the strings playing triads and 7th chords in root position – creating a stronger and firmer harmony

Extract 2

Listen especially for the way the theme develops and its treatment by the composer

LISTEN FOR:

- theme 1 played quietly by the trumpets with the last phrase of theme 2 played by muted strings in juxtaposition above. The whole is much slower and gentler, but maintains dignity – the word *nobile* appears in the brass instruments' parts

- the intervals in theme 1 expanding (up to an octave and beyond)

- the harmonies growing darker and more complex in the chords from the strings that sustain the theme

- the pedal notes contributing to the tension as the music increases in dynamics

- about one second before the music returns to the tonic, the melody features one foreign note (A natural), which is repeated

- the tonic pedal note in the few bars before the cadential chords

- tonic and dominant notes from the timpani

- the cadential chords and dramatic rests causing the deafening silences at the end of the finale and symphony.

> *There is a great vastness in his symphonies and his music in general that confirms his pride and love for his country.*

FURTHER LISTENING:
Sibelius: *Tapiola*
Nielsen: *Symphony No. 4, Inextinguishable*

BÉLA BARTÓK
1881-1945 (Hungary)

Béla Bartók was born in Hungary, in a small town which is now part of Romania. He was a gifted musician from a very early age and although his ambition was to go to Vienna to study further, he was advised to attend the Music Academy in Budapest. Had he chosen to go to Vienna, his musical career would probably have turned out very differently.

Bartók and his friend, the Hungarian musician Zoltán Kodály, travelled extensively to remote parts of Hungary, Romania, Slovakia and Transylvania recording thousands of native songs. In his music, he generally avoided quoting these songs in their entirety, choosing instead to draw on the essential traits of the melodies. The influence of Wagner can sometimes be seen on his colourful instrumentation, and he was also drawn to Debussy's music - its modal elements, its new harmonies and its irregular rhythms. His work can be studied from several perspectives, but what makes his music unique is the prominent influence of his own country's folk music.

Dance Suite – No. 3

Full orchestra

He composed the Dance Suite in 1923 to celebrate the fiftieth anniversary of Budapest as a city in its new form. It is an attractive work, full of exuberant rhythms, colourful instrumentation and modal-flavoured harmonies. It comprises six movements, all tied together by a *ritornello*. This theme, first heard in the opening Dance, develops throughout the whole work and reflects the Verbunkos, a folk dance associated with the violin music of the Magyar, the Hungarian gypsies.

The third dance is in ABACA Rondo form, and the main theme is a development of the ritornello, echoing Hungarian bagpipe music.

A

bassoon

LISTEN FOR:

- the bassoon in its upper register imitating the sound of bagpipes

- the pentatonic mode B-C#-E-F#-A-B with its emphasis on 4ths (B-E, E-A, F#-B)

Petatonic mode or scale on white notes

- drone accompaniment on tonic and dominant by horns and piano

- syncopated pizzicato by the strings

- the way the clarinet and strings repeat the theme using the instruments' different colours to vary the melody

- the change in the accompaniment from pizzicato to ar*co* by the strings

- acciacatura on the main notes of the melody from time to time creating a folky feel to the music

- the climax of the main theme as the melody is developed in inversions, with the flute playing trills to create agitation, and glissandi by the strings

- at the climax, note how the rhythms become slightly more irregular and syncopated

- the section ends with open 4ths from the strings

B

Theme B is heard immediately after an allargando.
It is in a Romanian folk violin style.

LISTEN FOR:

- the change of time signature in every bar to create rhythmic interest
- the generally diatonic tonality, suggesting G major but with the sharpened 4th (C#) which gives us a flavour of Lydian or Eastern modes – a prominent feature of Bartok's musical language
- a drone of G and D (tonic and dominant) by the lower strings and wind as accompaniment
- the open 5ths (D and A) on the open strings in the melody
- the piccolo joining the strings to play the main melody
- a short musical dialogue between the oboe and cor anglais – reed instruments imitating the sound of traditional instruments
- the celesta and harp play quick runs and glissandi, giving the sound yet another colour

A1

The main theme returns.

LISTEN FOR:

- the piccolo joining the bassoon which is an octave below
- the piano is heard more clearly, and used almost as a percussion instrument, i.e. not melodically as in the nineteenth century
- *campanelli*, bells (or glockenspiel) and cymbals creating a more unusual sound and playing a variation on the main theme
- the tonic and dominant notes (B and F#) are given more prominence than in the preceding section
- the section is much shorter

C

The melody heard in the second episode also reflects Romanian violin music.

LISTEN FOR:

- the slower tempo in order to create variety
- the very similar tonality to section B but with the 7th note of the scale flattened this time, F natural, keeping the sharpened 4th, the C#
- the alternating pizzicato and arco from the violins highlighting the traditional open-stringed method of playing by the first violin (*non div* in the score)
- the following short scherzando suggests E flat tonality but in the Mixolydian mode (with flattened 7th) and extensive use is made of 4ths in the sequences and chords.

These motifs also echo the main theme. This demonstrates Bartók's craft as a Neo-Classical composer, but still weaving folk characteristics into his music.

A2

The main theme returns for the last time.

LISTEN FOR:

- the quicker tempo creating an effective finale
- the flexibility of time – a slight slowing down before ending the dance in lively fashion in open 5ths and 4ths

> **FURTHER LISTENING:**
> Bartok: *Sonata for Two Pianos and Percussion*
> Kodaly: *Psalmus Hungaricus*

LEOŠ JANÁČEK
1854 -1928 (Czechoslovakia)

Janáček came to prominence and maturity as a recognised international composer late in life. He was in his forties before finding his own individual style and voice, and most of his works that have stood the test of time were composed in the twentieth century. He was born in Hukvaldy, Moravia, and received his early education as a member of the church choir in Brno, Czechoslovakia's second largest city, before going on to Prague, Leipzig and Vienna to study.

Janáček's important early contribution was to collect traditional Moravian songs and melodies. Though he quoted very little of the actual melodies, the characteristics of the folk music were evident in his own works. He concentrated mainly on trying to imitate the speech patterns of the Czech language, and so it is no surprise that he is chiefly remembered today for his seven operas, with *Jenůfa* (1904) being the most well-known.
He was obviously a patriotic man with a deep love of his country and its traditions. At the end of the First World War, Czechoslovakia won its independence, and some say that this is what inspired him to write so much towards the end of his life. He was also deeply in love with a twenty-five-year-old girl called Kamila Stösslová.

Janáček is known as a nationalist composer for a number of reasons. One of them is the fact that he used the vernacular of the language in his melodies and the characteristics of the folk song in his music. Secondly, his works contain many references to the country's old ways and folklore. Lastly, his compositions contain a great deal of celebratory spirit - as the composer said when Czechoslovakia gained its independence: "Here we are now - the heart of Europe. And that heart should be heard beating loudly"

Slava (Gloria) from the *Mša Glagolskaja* (Glagolitic Mass)

Choir, orchestra & soloists

This work, composed in 1926 (when Janáček was in his seventies) uses the old Slavonic language of the Church and employs the Glagolytic alphabet. This Mass is also regarded as a celebration of Slavonic culture and - like all his late works - is associated with the composer's love for Kamila Stösslová.

The Mass is the Catholic church service, but Janáček was not a religious man - he repeatedly claimed that he was an atheist despite spending time as a church choral scholar when he was twelve. Nevertheless, the fact that he had discovered the text written in the ancient script appealed to his nationalism. The work is full of exuberance - happy and jubilant fanfares alternating with energetic solos. This work is considered one of the composer's masterpieces.

The Mass

The Mass is the Catholic Church service. Some composers have used the words spoken in the service and set them to music. The mass then becomes a concert hall piece as in Beethoven's *Missa Solemnis* or Verdi's *Requiem Mass*.

The mass has a number of sections:

Kyrie Eleison	- asking for God's mercy
Gloria	- triumphantly praising God in the highest
Credo	- declaring the Christian beliefs
Sanctus	- praising God and meditating
Agnus Dei	- describing the gentleness of Jesus Christ

Each section has its own character.

LISTEN FOR:

- the strings in a very high register with bells illustrating the word *highest* in the lyrics and preparing the listener for the ensuing solo
- a soprano solo in a high register singing a melody based on triads or repeated notes. The rhythms do not match the rhythms in the accompaniment. Remember that Janáček liked to imitate the rhythms of everyday Czech speech.

- the accompaniment by clarinet, harp in broken chords, and strings with sustain notes creating a silvery sound
- an imitation or answer by the accompaniment, using the same short musical phrase as the soprano
- an instrumental interlude with a modal melody by the horns characterised by the interval of a 5th

- flutes and violins answering with the intervals now extended to 6ths
- shortly before the return of the soprano the instrumental interlude with 4-against-3 rhythms, adding to the gusto
- the first appearance of the mixed choir, singing three-bar phrases. They sing a development of what the soprano sang when she was first heard. A progression of the entry occurs after two bars' accompaniment, a 3rd higher, and somewhat developed
- the second instrumental interlude. It includes busy little motifs from the strings and flute based on the accompaniment heard at the opening of the section. They resemble ostinati, and include a number of progressions
- the end of the instrumental interlude. The choir motif is heard from the trombones
- a new entry by the choir. The words *"Chvalim Te"* start a new section of rejoicing. The texture is dense here, with instrumental sections consolidating the voices and harmony matching the words. There is also a jubilant transposition to Bb major in the instrumental music

- another new section, where the soprano sings the words *Bože otče vsemogyj*. Here again, the same material, repeated notes, is used. Between entries, the interval of a 5th is very prominent in the orchestral part
- the choir's entry singing in antiphonal 'question and answer' style with the male answering the female voices. The accompaniment echoes many of the motifs heard previously
- ostinato from the brass accompanied by the timpani to close the section.

Follow the words as you listen.

Slava vo vyšnich Bogu i na zeml'i mir človekom
blagovol'enja.
Chvalim Te, blagoslavl'ajem Te, klanajem Ti se,
slavoslovim Te.
Chvali vozdajem Tebĕvelikyje radi slavy tvojeje.
Bože, otče vsemogyj,
Gospodi synu jedinorodnyj,
Isuse Chrste!

Glory to God on high,
and on earth peace to men of good will.
We praise thee, We bless thee,
We adore thee, We glorify thee.
We give thanks to thee for thy great glory,
O Lord God, heavenly king,
God the Father almighty,
Jesus Christ.

Janáček once said that the work was inspired by a thunderstorm. "The sky turned black, and I similarly thought of the *Kyrie Eleison* asking for mercy. Then the lightning flashed and the *Gloria* in *Excelsis* was composed in my head. And finally, the *Sanctus* and *Agnus Dei*. The calm after the storm"

National characteristics in Janáček's music deriving from his study of the country's folk music:

- the everyday spoken Slavonic language is reflected in the fact that many sections resemble recitatives in his melodies
- irregular rhythms
- small motifs repeated in progressions or inversions
- the unexpected patterns of his melodies and irregular phrasing
- many ostinati (Janáček was called the first minimalist)
- joyful sections alternating with extremely mournful sections (reflecting the political situation as well as the composer's personal situation)

FURTHER LISTENING:

Janáček: *Sinfonietta*
Martinu: *The Frescoes of Pierro della Francesca*

RALPH VAUGHAN WILLIAMS
1872-1958 (England)

Many consider Vaughan Williams to be England's greatest composer since Henry Purcell. In a long career, he composed powerful and majestic music, full of expression and inspiring pride in English hearts. He was educated in Cambridge and London, but in his late thirties, he went to Paris to study with Ravel. From then on, he felt that his own individual art and voice as a composer were on firmer foundations, and he kept on composing until his death.

He was born in the village of Down Ampney in Gloucesterhire but his father died when he was a year old and he grew up at Leith Hill Place in Surrey, his mother's home. He was interested in English folk songs, but didn't start to collect them until he was in his thirties. This element had struck a sensitive chord in his heart almost ten years earlier when he came across a book called *English Country Songs*:

"I had that sense of recognition - here's something which I have known all my life, only I didn't know it".

Fantasia on a Theme by Thomas Tallis

full orchestra, chamber orchestra and string quartet

As well as including folk songs and their characteristics in his music, he had another mission. Vaughan Williams believed that English music's golden age had been the Tudor and Elizabethan age - the Renaissance period - with its rich polyphony and colourful modes. He went back to that era to seek inspiration, and found it largely in the music of Thomas Tallis who was born around 1500. He found church music by Tallis - motets and anthems, one or two madrigals and music for instruments such as the viol, organ and virginals (a kind of early harpsichord).

He also discovered nine psalm-tunes, the third of which he used for the Fantasia. He composed the work in 1910 and revised it in 1913 and 1920.

What makes the *Fantasia* a magnificent work is the way Vaughan Williams treats the melody of the psalm tune. For instance, so many changes in dynamics and tempi would not be seen in the Renaissance model, neither would phrases connecting one section to another be seen. It was composed for the Three Choirs Festival and first performed in the vast space of Gloucester Cathedral.

The result is the *Fantasia*, a piece which is quite personal and original in style.

It varies emotionally - from the cold to the passionate, from the tranquil to the dramatic - and is a work that gripped the imagination and soul of the English from the start.

General features:

- the work is for three groups of stringed instruments - full orchestra; a smaller orchestra of nine instruments acting as a kind of echo for the larger one; and a string quartet, made up of the leaders of all four string sections of the full orchestra. This recalls groupings like Gabrieli's *Sonata Pian' e Forte* or the ripieno/concertino in the Baroque Concerto Grosso

- the term 'Fantasia' comes from the Renaissance Period. At the time it meant a piece composed in free structure, without encumbrance of form or a definite plan. These features are found in this piece, which calls to mind the Elizabethan fantasia for viols.

- the second half of Tallis's theme is in the Phrygian mode (E-E) for several bars.

Vaughan Williams said that the ecclesiastical modes released him from the harmonic cul-de-sac that existed in Western music at the time

- there are two main ideas here - Tallis's theme and a motif that sways back and forth around one note; the entire work has grown from these two

LISTEN FOR:

- Tallis's theme (A) divided into four and punctuated from time to time by a second motif (B)

- Another motif, (B) between snippets of Tallis's melody. This was originally part of the melody but Vaughan Williams has accorded it the function of an active motif, moving from one section to the other and punctuating the music every now and then. It is also gloriously harmonised with a false relation. It sways to and fro around one note in the tradition of the modal plainsongs from the Middle Ages

- a tremolo from the strings as a sound-silvering device – Vaughan Williams's 'magic chords' as they are known by some
- imitation in the large orchestra between the highest and lowest string instruments using figure Ai. Polyphony becomes an integral part of the Fantasia later on
- antiphony (dialogue or 'question and answer') between two orchestras. The smaller orchestra is traditionally set apart from the large orchestra so that the sound reaches the listener's ears as an echo
- the extreme difference in dynamics between sections. This is due to the different sizes of the orchestras as well as the dynamics marks
- the solo by the viola from the string quartet at the end of the extract that derives from Aiii which eventually develops into imitative entries

FURTHER LISTENING:
Vaughan Williams: *The Lark Ascending*
Holst: *The Planets*

NATIONALISM

AARON COPLAND
1900 -1990 (USA)

Aaron Copland is considered one of the USA's major twentieth century composers, mainly because he succeeded in encapsulating the American psyche and character. Because of its ability to delve into the American subconscious, his music has been used in a variety of television advertisements. He is sometimes called 'the cowboy composer' or the 'Wild West composer' since his music depicts that way of life so vividly. As a child, his mother used to sing cowboy songs to him and before composing the pieces influenced by rural America, he spent time in areas such as Santa Fe and South California.

Hoe-Down from the ballet *Rodeo*   Full orchestra

During World War II, the Ballet Russe de Monte Carlo made its home in New York, and the new choreographer, Agnes de Mille, was eager to stage *Rodeo*, a ballet about cowboys. When Copland was offered the job he was a little apprehensive, having already composed music for a similar ballet, *Billy the Kid*. But he accepted the offer, promising to himself that *Rodeo* would be different to the earlier work. Following the plot of *Rodeo*, Copland divided his score into five sections, with the *Hoe-Down* at the end. He completed the work in 1942.

The scenes take place outside the barn of a typical American ranch, and contain extremely suggestive dances, portraying girls enthusiastically flirting and men responding! As one critic said, "I don't know why *Rodeo* hasn't been denounced and picketed by women's liberationists". The *Hoe-Down* is like an American flamenco, with couples dancing energetically and sexually, spiritedly challenging each other. This is reflected in the music. Copland also used a number of folk songs from a book *Traditional Music of America*, namely the fiddle tunes *Mc Leod's Reel* and *Bonyparte*, and also *Gilderoy* and *Tip Toe, Pretty Fairy*, airs often heard in Scottish ceilidhs.

The USA is a young country, still trying to establish a unique identity. As a result, the influences on its music are varied and wide, drawing from numerous European and Latin-American sources. *Rodeo* presents the white people's music, reflecting the traditions of immigrants from countries such as Ireland and Scotland.

Hoe-Down's musical material reflects an informal folk session, as the opening music imitates a group of musicians tuning up. Then comes a feeling of enormous release, as the main theme pushes forward relentlessly and includes ornaments similar to those heard in Scottish and Irish fiddle music and folk songs. There are contrasting melodies, slightly less frantic, in the middle section, before the main theme returns at the end, in *fff* to close the piece and the whole work. Certain characteristics can be heard that are very common in traditional music, but which now contribute to the new Wild West tradition in the USA.

LISTEN FOR:

Rhythmic features:

- ostinati and repetition
- sustained, relentless rhythm with many semiquavers and the main accent emphasised
- rhythmic vamping
- rhythm that reflects tap-dancing or Celtic reel dancing
- a relaxation of rhythm and a decrease in tempo towards the middle as the flirting turns into kissing in the scene on stage
- regular eight-bar melodies
- many accents and emphasis on certain notes
- bluegrass style is evident
- the slight accelerando towards the end in most performances which emphasises the relentless element in the music

Melodic and harmonic features that reflect folk music:

- pentatonic scales in the main melody

- the frequent use of chords I and V
- drone and pedal notes treated in various ways

- vamping by the piano, with alternative bass notes, possibly to increase the interest in the dance steps

- open 5ths grouped together – not necessarily the same notes

- Aeolian modal features in the melody heard in the middle section by the oboe (A minor with G natural)

- Octave leaps, despite the melodies' relatively limited range
- keys like D and G major, which suit the open strings of the stringed instruments
- a pedal note for many bars towards the end to bring the music to an exciting climax
- an element of question and answer in the middle section imitating the competitive mood between the two dancers
- the ornaments in the first bar in the main melody reflecting Scottish and Irish folk fiddle-playing styles

Instrumentation:

- the violin is central to the piece, reflecting traditional music, especially as the symbol ° denotes that some notes are to be played on open strings to obtain a raw, more folky sound
- the xylophone gives a flash of sound at climaxes and in the main theme, emphasising the pentatonic element in the melody
- wooden blocks are used to imitate horses' hooves, a prominent feature of New World music
- the trumpet maintains the brilliance in the middle section although the melody is slightly less rousing
- heavier instruments like the trombone and double bass play pedal notes add to the tension of the work
- the banjo's influence or style has permeated a number of the work's ostinati
- the use of the piano as an orchestral instrument

FURTHER LISTENING:
Copland: *Appalachian Spring*
Barber: *Knoxville, 1915*

GRACE WILLIAMS
1906-1977 (Wales)

Grace Williams, one of Wales's most influential twentieth-century composers, was born in Glamorgan, South Wales. Her parents were eager to see her study music, but not in the conventional academic sense through books and examinations. Her father was a highly-respected choral conductor who simply opened up his library to his daughter and left her to find her own path. In 1923 she won a scholarship to study music at the University in Cardiff, but the academic nature of the course was not to her liking and she used to escape back to her home town of Barry to compose music, looking out at the sea. In 1926 she entered the Royal College of Music in London where her most influential teacher was Ralph Vaughan Williams.

After a period of study in Vienna, where she became familiar with the work of Mahler, Wagner and Richard Strauss, she returned to England and took up a teaching post at a public school for girls in London. Here, she started composing in earnest. One of her pieces often performed at the time was *Hen Walia* (Old Walls), based on a Welsh lullaby. Throughout her career, Welsh music was a significant part of her creative output – she used several folk songs and some unique Welsh features such as penillion singing as a base for her compositions.

Ironically, her most prolific period coincided with the Second World War. Her *Fantasia on Welsh Nursery Tunes* (1941), based on eight tunes, became her best-known and most enduring work despite the fact that Grace Williams herself did not rate the work highly. At the end of the war, she returned to Wales. She felt that her compositions were not sufficiently individualistic to raise her above other composers, and she searched long and hard for a voice she could call her own. In her later years she composed more developed works such as *Penillion*, *Carillons* the Trumpet Concerto and *The Dancers*, a substantial choral series which recognised and paid tribute to her country's vocal tradition. She died of cancer in 1977, at peace and quietly satisfied that she had made a significant contribution to Welsh music.

High Wind from *Sea Sketches*

String orchestra

The sea had always been an inspiration to Grace Williams. When her school in Camden was forced to move to Lincolnshire during the war, she longed for the sea. *Sea Sketches* was composed in 1944 and she dedicated the work to her parents "who had the good sense to set up home on the coast of Glamorgan." The work was written when the Second World War was drawing to its close. It is now recognised that she was influenced at this time by English composers such as Elgar, Vaughan Williams and Delius who all had one thing in common – their liking for string music. Grace Williams had learnt to play the violin at school and *Sea Sketches* shows an obvious understanding of the string family. She said that this work had been written in chamber orchestra style since counterpoint plays such a prominent part.

The five movements paint lively and spirited pictures of the Glamorgan coast in a variety of moods. In the first, *High Wind*, the little themes appear like the spray of crashing waves, while the second, *Sailing Song*, is more serene. In the third, *Channel Sirens,* the sounds of ships' warning horns are imitated and *Breakers* is like a wild scherzo. The work closes with the serene and tranquil last movement, *Calm Sea in Summer*.

Although Grace Williams used folk songs in her work, this piece does not display any particular folk characteristics. What makes her a 'national' composer here is her effort to portray the country's landscape in her music and the fact that she was inspired by her native land

FURTHER LISTENING:
Grace Williams: *Penillion*
Hoddinott: *Symphony No. 6*

High Wind falls into three main parts:

The first section. Introduction of themes.

LISTEN FOR:

- the two opening ideas. The first is the demi-semiquaver motif (A) by the viola and half the second violin section (the strings are frequently split)

- the second idea (B) – the theme heard by the high strings (the other half of the second violins and the first violin). The harmony is diatonic, and the three string instruments which play the theme form triads, either in the root position or inversion. There is also an element of parallel movement in semitones, a feature which will grow in importance later on in the movement as the music becomes more chromatic

- imitation between the high and low strings with the following motif, the third main idea (C), which originates after all from the second part of theme B

- the irregular syncopated rhythms as theme B is developed the pizzicato by the low strings giving the music a new sparkle and pushing it forward
- the tremolos by the low strings while the theme is being developed by the high strings in order to convey the continual swirling of the wind
- the developing of the second part of theme B – semiquavers developing into triplets in order to create irregular rhythms. These triplets will be heard regularly during the movement, and will be used to create friction with the fixed quavers – often two against three

- the triplet feature becoming ever more prominent as the section draws to a close and a rest appearing at the beginning of each group making it sound like an appogiatura

The middle section. Developing the themes.

LISTEN FOR:

- the leap from the major 8th and 7th in the music by the high strings
- the main theme's intervals becoming wider
- the musical language becoming slightly more chromatic and the semitone element becoming more prominent in the melody
- the climax where all the instruments play homophonically in unison triplets before starting the last section

The last section. Returning to the opening theme but still developing.

LISTEN FOR:

- the opening theme (B) returning first of all in the cellos which split into three solos, giving the music an air of mystery due to the lower pitch and the thinner texture
- the same theme being passed over to the high instruments, once again in chords
- an element of compressing ideas so that the motifs and themes become shorter, giving the music a sense of urgency
- the appogiatura idea becoming more and more prominent in the high-pitched instruments
- all the instruments playing theme C very loudly to create a climax
- the way Grace Williams closes the movement quietly after the storm and finally anchors playing the theme C.
- the key of C major with the cellos playing pedal notes on the tonic and the double basses playing tonic and dominant notes in _pizzicato_

DMITRI SHOSTAKOVICH
1906-1975 (Soviet Union)

"Amid the conflicting pressures of official requirements, the mass suffering of his fellow countrymen, and his personal ideals of humanitarian and public service, he succeeded in forging a musical language of colossal emotional power." (Grove Dictionary)

Following the centenary celebrations of his birth in 2006, Shostakovich seems to have emerged as one of the most important and influential composers of the twentieth century, as well as one of the most popular. The wide ranging appeal of his music has been embraced by the public in the wake of the 1987 film *Testimony*, based on his life and starring Ben Kingsley, where his complex relationship with the Communist Party in the Soviet Union was portrayed, and also the short clips of his music in films such as *Eyes Wide Shut* (Kubric) in 1999. He is widely regarded as a 'nationalist' composer but also with strong elements of Neo-Classicism in his music.

Shostakovich was born in St. Petersburg, Russia. He soon made his mark as an exceptionally gifted child, astonishing everyone with his piano performances. Having studied under the composer Glazunov, he graduated in the St Petersburg Conservatoire and used his First Symphony in 1926 as his graduating composition. Ironically, however, he failed his compulsory examination on Marxist methodology in the same year.

From that point, his relationship with the Communist Party was erratic. He didn't join the Party until his late fifties, and it has been suggested that he had been bribed before doing so. His music (his opera *The Lady Macbeth of the Mtsensk District*, 1934, in particular) was criticised harshly in the 30s because it contained references to a way of life which the Communists detested. In response, Shostakovich wrote his Fifth Symphony and included a written apology on the title page. Complex and innovative music was condemned because it was out of reach of the common people, and for most of his life, Shostakovich's music oscillated between what was acceptable to the Communists and what he as a composer wished to create. Despite all this, however, he is regarded as a 'nationalist' composer because of the large number of works he composed that had political overtones. For example, the Seventh Symphony is called *Leningrad* and Stalin himself is portrayed in the Tenth Symphony's scherzo.

Piano Trio no. 2 in E minor op. 67 – Finale

Piano, violin & cello

The work was written in 1944. The finale includes a *totentanz*, a Death Dance, and there are strong Jewish elements in the music. The attitude of the Soviet Union towards Jews had varied during the twentieth century, but many adopted a sympathetic attitude. Shostakovich composed several pieces which included references to the Jews. He set Jewish folk poems to music in a song-cycle (1948) and he wrote his Thirteenth Symphony in 1962 to commemorate the 1941 Babi Yar massacre in the Ukraine, where around 100,000 Jews were shot in the space of just two days.

Prominent features in Jewish music:

- lively dance music – with fiddle and gypsy music prominent
- at other times, extremely sad music; the words very often depicting the story of the Jews
- music based on the *Ahava Rabboh* mode or scale, also called the *Phrygian dominant scale*. The main features of this scale is the flattened 2nd degree, and the sharpened 3rd, thus creating an augmented interval between the 2nd and 3rd note. It also corresponds to the harmonic minor scale, starting on the dominant note of that scale (imagine starting off on the 5th note of the F minor harmonic scale as seen below).

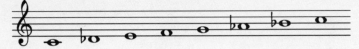

The music is in Rondo form and includes Sonata form features (see the chapter on the Concerto for Double String Orchestra, Third Movement by Tippett).

Rondo Form - A B A C A etc. with the main theme returning several times.

Theme A

LISTEN FOR:

- pedal notes being repeated by the piano in octaves on the dominant note, B
- the main theme played pizzicato by the violin, where the augmented 2nd interval is prominent – in this case between the F♮ and the D♯

- the unusual cadence, modulating to B major at the end of the first appearance of the theme
- the cello notes when the main theme is heard for the second time, again playing pizzicato, repeating the two tonic notes and the leading note, thus drawing attention to the semitone interval
- the modulation at the end of this section – this time to F♯ major

Theme B

LISTEN FOR:

- the semitone interval which becomes more prominent between the F♯ and the G♮ natural played by the piano

- the oom-pah accompaniment by the cello and violin – still pizzicato, but both instruments playing four-note chords across the four strings. The theme is repeated quietly and becomes louder towards the end.

FURTHER LISTENING:
Shostakovich: *Symphony No. 7 (Leningrad)*
Prokofiev: *Alexander Nevsky*

Theme A1

LISTEN FOR:

- the violing playing *arco* (with the bow) this time, adding a few slurs to convey the gypsy fiddle style
- the harmonies, expanded and changed
- the oom-pah accompaniment between the piano and cello this time
- a slight development of the main theme towards the end of the section when the last bars of the theme are used in repetitions and sequences
- the music increasing in intensity and emotion

Theme C

LISTEN FOR:

- the *espressivo* theme by the cello in irregular time and in a high range. It is all built on semitones.

- short sections of theme A and B interwoven with theme C
- the repetition of theme C with a countermelody in the piano

Theme A2

LISTEN FOR:

- the main theme returning very softly in the lower notes of the piano with syncopated chords by the two string instruments

Characteristics of Shostakovich as a nationalist composer

- frequent use of Russian folk melodies
- use of political events as a basis for his compositions, often using titles for his works based on major events in the Soviet Union

Neo-classical characteristics

- several works making use of classical forms such as symphony, sonata, concerto and string trios and quartets
- the form and structure of his compositions are easy to recognise and to analyse

CHARLES IVES
1874-1954 (USA)

Charles Ives is now considered to be the USA's first significant composer, but his music lay forgotten for many years and was not performed. Today, however, he is regarded as one of the most original American composers, combining innovative ideas with the spirit of the 'New Land'.

He was born in Connecticut, New England and much of his work is based on the experiences of his youth. His father was an unconventional brass band leader and the young Ives was strongly encouraged to take an interest in music that broke new ground. Ives was shown the rudiments of bitonality and polytonality by his father who would often play melodies on the piano and encourage Charles to play an accompaniment in another key. At fourteen years old, he was a church organist and had started composing. He also played the piano, drums and cornet.

When Ives went to Yale University in 1893, he came under the influence of Horatio Parker, and started to write choral and church music like his mentor. A year later his father died, a heavy blow for the young man. He decided to carry on composing in the same adventurous style that his father was so fond of, and continued to experiment musically as a kind of tribute.

Ives wasn't a healthy man, and in 1907, he suffered what he took to be a heart attack. It is now thought that these attacks were to a degree psychological, but it was after this first attack that he began his most productive period as a composer. Despite following a very successful career in insurance, he continued to compose prolifically until he suffered another attack in 1918. Ives wrote his last composition, the song *Sunrise*, in 1926, but he carried on revising and refining his music. He died in New York in 1954.

Symphony no. 3
The Camp Meeting –
3rd movement

Full orchestra but with chamber elements – one of each woodwind and brass (but two horns)

Among the first influences on Charles Ives's music was the open air concerts he would hear in his home town, Danbury. As a result, he had a broad repertoire from the world of popular tunes, brass band marches and hymns - fragments of Americana which he used extensively in his works later on.

The Third Symphony was written in 1914 but was later edited. It combines what Ives the organist knew about counterpoint and Bach's compositions with the experiences he had gained in the evangelical meetings of his youth. At these meetings, his father had provided the music and conducted the congregational singing. The last movement, *Communion*, uses the hymn tune *What a Friend we Have in Jesus*, but treats it very differently. In the 1930s, the composer Lou Harrison brought Ives's work to the ears of a wider audience, and it was he who conducted its first performance in 1946. In 1947, Ives was awarded the Pulitzer prize for the symphony, which brought him out of the shadows to international status.

Before listening

• The movement is based on the hymn tune *Woodworth*, with a paraphrase of another hymn tune *Azmon* as countermelody

- The form shows Ives as an innovator in the world of composition. It combines such traditional forms as Air and Variations with the idea of symphonic development. Small fragments of the melody are heard here and there throughout the movement until it is heard in its entirety at the end. This is different to the usual practice of announcing a theme at the beginning and then developing it later as was the norm among European composers.

General features in the music of Charles Ives

The main feature is the striking contrast between the simple 'borrowed' musical material and the musical complexity that surrounds it. Listen in general for the following:

- many American tunes such as marches, popular rag music, and hymns treated in quite different ways
- bitonality - a melody in one key with accompaniment in another key
- polytonality - a number of keys played simultaneously
- quarter tones - intervals smaller than semitones
- cluster chords, often used in parallel
- chords based on 4ths
- two rhythmic patterns heard simultaneously, one slower than the other
- irregular rhythms, without a sense of any regular beat in the bar
- bars of different times following each other or bars without any time signature at all
- instruments from the more popular world of music such as brass bands combined with conventional orchestral instruments

As we listen, there are three prominent statements of the hymn tune Woodworth.

LISTEN FOR:

the version by the violins

- the notes in a very high range playing only parts of the hymn tune. The rhythms are not the same but the outline is quite clear. The first three notes of the theme are all-important as they are played many times in the remainder of the movement by various instruments

- the way the hymn tune in this statement receives a treatment which is remarkably similar to the choral prelude. Ives, being an organist, would have been very comfortable in the genre
- the generally diatonic, triadic harmony that accompanies the hymn tune, but in an unexpected sequence, with chords that are distant in pitch following each other, e.g. a Bb major chord moving to D major, or E minor moving to Gb major, forming parallel triads
- the return of the first three notes of the theme before the end of the rendition

the version by the horns

- more of the hymn tune than in the previous extract

- the thinner texture this time, with the strings playing very quietly
- the darker harmonies creating a more intense atmosphere
- versions of the first three notes of the theme appearing frequently after the theme by the horns the texture increasing in density as the brass instruments consolidate the sound
- the increasing dynamics and slight acceleration before the last version – the word *stringendo* is marked in the score
- a solo flute leading us into the last rendition

the version by the solo cello

- one redundant entry before the hymn tune is heard in its entirety from the cello
- a paraphrase of the hymn tune *Azmon* is heard as a countermelody above the cello by violin 1 and another little countermelody is played by the bassoon
- the texture, though quiet, is very busy with demisemiquavers by the viola
- *pizzicato* from the lower strings – this lightens the texture somewhat
- the texture becoming increasingly homophonic towards the end, as the work comes to a close
- the barely audible church bells at the end, and the strings played *ppp*

FURTHER LISTENING:
Ives: *Three Places in New England*
Carter: *A Symphony of Three Orchestras*

OLIVIER MESSIAEN
1908-1992 (France)

Messiaen was born in Provence, France. At eleven years old, having already begun a successful musical career, he enrolled as a student at the Conservatoire, Paris. He was soon appointed organist at La Trinité church in Paris, but during the Second World War he was called up as a medical auxiliary in the French army and was imprisoned by the Nazis. Later in his life, he taught musicians like Boulez and Stockhausen. He was a committed Catholic and much of his music derives directly from his religion.

Messiaen is considered to be one of the greatest French composers of the twentieth century. He was influenced very early in his career by the music of Debussy and the characteristics are evident in colourful orchestration, modal and unexpected harmony and non-metrical rhythms. He was also fascinated by Indian music, and many *ragas* and *thalas* from Hindu music appear in his work. Perhaps one of the most interesting things about Messiaen is that he liked to include transcriptions of birdsong in his music, and there are many photographs of him in the fields near his home noting birdsongs.

La Navitité du Seigneur -

Nine meditations for organ. No. 9 : Dieu parmi nous

Large pipe organ with several manuals

Two elements in the work *La Navitité du Seigneur* (the Birth of our Lord) need explaining.

1) Messiaen invented different and original 'scales' for his own purposes and called them "modes of limited transposition". These are scales that enable him to treat harmony in very unconventional ways – and many of them have some kind of mystic symbolism as well. The scales include Hindu music intervals as a prominent feature. The composer has also often built unconventional and atonal chords on the individual notes.

2) During his time in a concentration camp during the war, Messiaen composed one of his best-known pieces, the *Quatuor Pour la Fin du Temps*, (Quartet for the End of Time), in which he broke new ground in rhythm and symbolism in music. One of these inventions was the *valeur ajouteé* or 'added value rhythms' in which he interrupts the regular metre of a musical phrase with short added length to one or more of the notes. The added length may take the form of an added dot, or a rest, or a note of little value, which intentionally causes the regular metre in the bar to go awry. So, in theory, there could be five and a quarter beats in the bar. Some believe that this is one of the great symbolisms of the Quartet as a work – the end of 'time' in music as we know it.

Both these elements existed in the Nine Meditations for organ, *La Navitité du Seigneur* composed in 1935, and reach a climax in the last of the meditations, *Dieu parmi nous* (God among us).

Symbolism in Messiaen's music

- atonal music is often a symbol of eternity
- music rooted in a tonal chord or normal tonality can represent the strength of the unchanging God or the incarnation of the trinity amongst earthly mortals
- ostinati or a repetitive rhythms often refer to an individual's captivity in sin, and the imitation of birdsong can refer to the freedom of the individual.

Track A

LISTEN FOR:

- the sequence in the two sets of chords that descend quickly at the start of the extract and convey eternity in their atonality. (G - Great Manual; P - Choir Manual; R - Swell Manual)

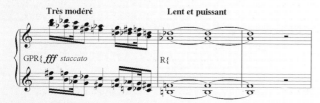

- the chords' direction suggests the incarnation coming 'down from heaven'. Note that there is no time signature here
- the powerful melody in the pedal after the chords, again a descending phrase, with the intervals getting closer as they reach the bottom

- the quieter, more mellow melody that is played after the opening chords with a slightly softer sound on the organ: representing God's love for his people. The organ sounds or pipes to be used are noted in detail on the score. See the added-value notes here denoted with a small cross

- the opening chords, repeated in a higher register
- the quick runs containing the added-value notes. See those notes again denoted with a small cross

Track B

LISTEN FOR:

- the tonality firmly rooted in E major. This was a key Messiaen often used when referring to the mystic qualities of the Christian faith
- the descending motif of the pedal, heard again under the joyous music in E major
- a hint of tonic pedal seems to be implied under the chromaticism of the last bars, creating a great and triumphal tension until the organ's release on the final chord – which is what the subconscious is eagerly awaiting
- the very last chord is an E major chord with an added major 6th

FURTHER LISTENING:
Messiaen: *Quartet for the End of Time*
Duruflé: *Requiem*

OTHERS

GEORGE GERSHWIN
1898-1937 (USA)

Nostalgic impressions of Jazz and American musicals spring to mind when we think of George Gershwin. He was severely criticised for including jazz and light melodies in some of his more 'serious' compositions, but in the 1920s works like *Rhapsody in Blue* and Piano Concerto in F were fast establishing themselves as worthy compositions for the concert hall whilst popular with the public at the same time.

Gershwin also had his supporters, eminent composers such as Ravel, Poulenc and Schoenberg. Indeed, Ravel admitted that he had modelled some of his works, such as the Piano Concerto in G and his Violin Sonata on Gershwin's work. Even so, Gershwin always felt that he had a foot in both camps and wasn't fulfilled by either.

The process of composing never came easy to Gershwin. He was born in Brooklyn, New York, the son of Russian and Jewish immigrants. He composed songs, with his brother Ira writing the lyrics. They soon attracted the attention of Broadway, and together they composed several musicals.

After spending time in Europe, Paris specifically, Gershwin composed a number of pieces for the concert hall, reflecting the influences of composers like Debussy, Ravel and Satie. It is said that he asked Ravel for lessons, to which the latter replied 'Why should you be a second-rate Ravel when you can be a first-rate Gershwin?'

An American in Paris

Full orchestra

The tone poem *An American in Paris* (1928) comes from this concert hall period, as do the *Rhapsody* and Concerto. It's a small cameo of the way Gershwin saw himself when he came to Europe for the first time - a tourist completely swallowed by an unfamiliar city. The piece contains such a variety of familiar kinds of music that the public took to it immediately. It has echoes of Jewish European music as well as the Afro-American music of Gershwin's home country. A film with the same title and songs by George and Ira Gershwin was made in 1951, with Gene Kelly in the starring role. It remains very popular to this day.

Extract 1

Allegretto Grazioso / Giocoso / Vivo / Con umore / Con brio

LISTEN FOR:

- the unromantic style that characterises the opening, in the style of the Frenchman Eric Satie and the group of French composers dubbed *Les Six*. They delighted in promoting satirical and ironic music, and rejected sentimentality
- the quirkiness of the atmosphere reflected in the cheeky acciacatura in the very first notes of the main melody

- the sounds of car horns contributing to the picture. Gershwin brought a couple of Paris taxi horns with him when he returned to America for the premiere of the work. The three notes appear frequently in the music, played by various instruments
- the lower brass instruments playing an alternative bass line with the syncopated chord notes from the horns in oompah style, reminiscent of American ragtime style

- the busy polyphonic texture, each instrument having its own interesting line portraying the revelry and variety of life
- the question and answer in the phrases which are derived from the filler notes in jazz music. Listen specifically for the quick repetitive notes of the trumpets and trombone, a figure that will develop in importance in the following bars when played by the full orchestra

- the xylophone's motif in three-beat patterns but in 2/4 time, reminding us again of ragtime style

- the syncopation by the percussion instruments adding to the excitement, and the syncopation from the top strings playing crotchet triplets
- a new motif (derived from the previous trumpet motif), first heard from the clarinets in a very high register and which develops into an orchestral *tutti* later on. It's extended for two bars by the strings at the end of the extract.

Extract 2

Andante ma con ritmo deciso

LISTEN FOR:

- blues notes (flattened 3rds and 7ths) in the beautiful trumpet melody — American blues music at its best

- the varied 'fill-in' sections at the end of each phrase in the above theme.

- the jazz and blues techniques in the repetition of the theme by the strings – such as glissandi from the violins and pizzicato from the double basses
- the obligato sections by the flutes and bass clarinet, similar to New Orleans jazz
- the obvious presence of the saxophone – an instrument from the world of jazz and Big Bands, not a traditional orchestral instrument.

FURTHER LISTENING:
Gershwin: *Porgy and Bess*
Bernstein: *West Side Story*

BENJAMIN BRITTEN
1913-1976 (England)

Benjamin Britten is considered one of the twentieth century's greatest British composers. His music, love of poetry and outlook on the society in which he lived conveyed a broad-minded person with deeply-held convictions, a person who avoided following contemporary trends. He continues to be a controversial figure for some because of his political beliefs. He was a committed pacifist, and had international, wide-ranging interests. The major theme in his works is the value of each individual, although that individual may often be on the periphery – a theme which is probably a reflection of his own life.

Britten was born in Suffolk and received composition lessons at a very young age from another English composer, Frank Bridge. Though he had plans to study with Alban Berg in Vienna, his family was opposed to his leaving Britain, and he studied at the Royal College in London. By his mid-twenties his music was increasingly coming to the public's attention. More importantly perhaps, this was when Britten met the tenor Peter Pears, who was to be his lifelong partner as well as musical collaborator.

During his lifetime, Britten wrote a lot of music based on poems by people such as Wilfred Owen, W.H. Auden and others who shared many of his political and social convictions. Among his most prominent works are the *War Requiem*, the Canticles, *Seven Sonnets of Michelangelo* and a number of arrangements of English folk songs. He composed the operas *Billy Budd* and *Peter Grimes* and also wrote music for film. In 1964, he was awarded the first American Aspen Award for his contribution to humanity, and in his acceptance speech, he took the opportunity to express his opinion on the function of the composer and his duty to society.

The Choirmaster's Burial
from the song-cycle *Winter Words*

`Voice and piano`

Britten wrote numerous works specifically for Peter Pears. One of these was the song cycle *Winter Words* which he wrote for voice and piano in 1953 to words by Thomas Hardy (1840-1928). The work was performed at the Leeds Music Festival, with Peter Pears singing and Britten accompanying. The song *The Choirmaster's Burial* is economic in material and compositional craft, and captures the ironic nostalgia conveyed in the poem, without becoming over-sentimental. The greatest influence here is the *English Hymnal*, as a hymn tune is quoted to match the words. The music also contains much satire and humour.

Verse 1. A description of the gentle choirmaster and his wish for some musicians to play at his graveside during his funeral, in accordance with the tradition of the poet's childhood

LISTEN FOR:

- the recitative element in the song, bearing in mind that Britten was a master at writing operas
- the hymn tune *Mount Ephraim*, matching the reference to it in the poem, quoted in the accompaniment throughout the first verse

- the hymn-tune quotation in accompaniment to the tenor's very free rhythm: polyphony recalling the traits of the choral prelude of the Baroque Period or even Renaissance Period polyphony
- the vocalist singing in such a free rhythm that the harmonies from the hymn tune don't always blend with the voice, and occasional discords occuring, often around the words *Mount Ephraim* – ironically intended
- the melismatic notes on the last word in the first verse, 'seraphim' (angel)

OTHERS

Verse 2. The Vicar's decision not to have musicians play by the grave in case the 'weather is unfavourable' (this practice was frowned upon by some in the Victorian church)

LISTEN FOR:

- the satirical and humorous little figure in the accompaniment to portray the vicar's misgivings about the weather — we hear fuss and fluster in the busy little dotted crotchet and semiquaver motifs

- the steady quavers in the left hand piano accompaniment to go with the words *To get through it faster / They buried the master / Without any tune*
- the monotonic notes repeated in chant style by the voice on the same words, portraying the vicar's indifference and determination not to hold the service outdoors

Verse 3. The Vicar's vision. At the dead of the next night, what should he see playing and singing by the grave of the old choirmaster but a group of musicians in the form of spectres in white gowns.

LISTEN FOR:

- the key change conveying the change in the spirit of the words
- the flourishing melodic leaps conveying the vivacity of the musicians' playing at the graveside on the words 'singing and playing' and becoming increasingly higher pitched
- the hymn tune, now decorated and including triplet rhythms against quavers
- the melisma again on the word 'choirmaster'
- the bold and challenging spirit in the music showing that the church's dislike of the practice of playing at gravesides has been undermined
- the unaccompanied recitative at the end on the words 'Such the tenor man told / When he had grown old' – the song ends as it started.

OTHERS

The Choirmaster's Burial by Thomas Hardy

He often would ask us
That, when he died,
After playing so many
To their last rest,
If out of us any
Should here abide,
And it would not task us,
We would with our lutes
Play over him
By his grave-brim
The psalm he liked best –
The one whose sense suits
"Mount Ephraim" –
And perhaps we should seem
To him, in Death's dream,
Like the seraphim.

As soon as I knew
That his spirit was gone
I thought this his due,
And spoke thereupon.
"I think", said the vicar,
"A read service quicker
Than viols out-of-doors
In these frosts and hoars.

That old-fashioned way
Requires a fine day,
And it seems to me
It had better not be."
Hence, that afternoon,
Though never knew he
That his wish could not be,
To get through it faster
They buried the master
Without any tune.

But 'twas said that, when
At the dead of next night
The vicar looked out,
There struck on his ken
Thronged roundabout,
Where the frost was graying
The headstoned grass,
A band all in white
Like the saints in church-glass,
Singing and playing
The ancient stave
By the choirmaster's grave.

Such the tenor man told
When he had grown old.

FURTHER LISTENING:
Britten: *War Requiem*
Walton: *Belshazzar's Feast*

WILLIAM MATHIAS
1934-1992 (Wales)

William Mathias was born in Whitland, Carmarthenshire in South West Wales. He studied at University of Wales, Aberystwyth, the Royal Academy in London, and in 1959 became a lecturer in the Music Department of the University of Wales, Bangor. After a short period in Edinburgh he returned to Bangor, and was Professor of Music there from 1970 to 1988.

His work varies from the enthusiastic and optimistic to the quiet and meditative. A particular awareness of the music of the Welsh people and the Celtic spirit are an integral part of his compositions. What makes him noteworthy are his versatility, his exceptional skills in writing for a variety of media, instrumental and vocal, and his deep understanding of the properties of various instruments and voices.

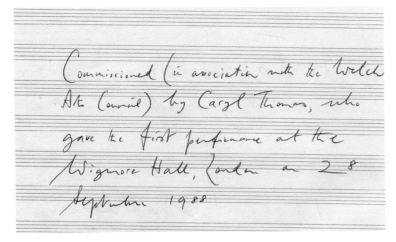

William Mathias's dedication to the harpist Caryl Thomas

Sun Dance from *Santa Fe Suite*

Harp Solo

The Welsh have a special affinity with the harp as their 'national instrument', and William Mathias was well aware of this. Already, before composing the *Santa Fe Suite* for harp, he had composed the *Improvisations* (1958) for his fellow student at the Royal Academy, the harpist David Watkins.

He also composed the Harp Concerto (1970) for Osian Ellis, and a Harp Sonata for the same harpist four years later. He wrote the *Santa Fe Suite* for the harpist Caryl Thomas in 1988, and it was performed for the first time at the Wigmore Hall in London in the same year.

William Mathias wasn't just a composer of 'Welsh' music. A year before composing this *Suite*, he'd visited Santa Fe in New Mexico and was enchanted by the landscape, the people and their customs. He attended a festival in Santa Fe where he experienced the colourful music of the Spanish and the native Americans, and watched a shaman from the Sioux Oglala tribe perform the ritualistic 'sun dance.'

A few days before William Mathias died four years later, the harpist Elinor Bennett visited his home to play the *Suite* for him. She remembers the composer, despite his ailing health, dancing with gusto around the room, recreating the shaman's performance in Santa Fe as a symbol of rebirth. She plays the Suite in the recording on the accompanying CD.

LISTEN FOR:

• the form – ABA

Section A

• the *acciacaturas* in the opening notes which create a light atmosphere from the start

• the scale used by the composer, (C# D E F G# A Bb) in the opening *glissando*, full of diminished and augmented seconds to create the appropriate mood. There are elements here too of the Phrygian mode, with the flattened 2nd in the scale (E-F natural), a mode which gives the music a Spanish feel.

• the rhythmic alternations between 6/8 and 3/4 which give bounce and vivacity to the music

• the open 5ths and 4ths superimposed onto each other in other chords – a prominent feature of Mathias's music in general, which creates a primitive, timeless feel

Section B

• a melody in 6/8 but with left-hand semiquavers in 2/4 time which creates a disturbance in the rhythm

• the suggestion of the tritone interval (F-B natural) and the minor 2nd in the accompaniment which is a prominent feature of this second melody in the middle section

• the harmonics, which create a transparent texture like little sunbeams in the music, and the glissandi, which enlighten the atmosphere

• the music rotating around one pivotal note developing into glissandi – a feature of the Spanish flamenco dance

Section A'

• the main melody's return, but with some changes, fuller in texture and with one episode of the middle section also included

Coda

• the pronounced accelerando as the dance reaches its climax, where the player uses the fingernails to create a more exciting sound

• the arpeggi on open 5ths before the final descending glissando with the fingernails

> **FURTHER LISTENING:**
> Mathias: *This Worlde's Joie*
> Geraint Lewis: *The Souls of the Righteous (in memoriam William Mathias)*

KARLHEINZ STOCKHAUSEN
b.1928 (Germany)

One of the most innovative and original composers of the twentieth century, Stockhausen was born in Burg Mödrath not far from Cologne, Germany. He studied at the Cologne College of Music, and at university there, before going on to study at Darmstadt University and then in Paris in the 1950s with composers Darius Milhaud and Olivier Messiaen. After completing a period studying acoustics in Bonn University, he returned to Darmstadt to lecture, and later lectured throughout Europe and North America. He admits that his work strays very far from traditional musical processes and his biggest influences are Messiaen and Anton Webern. His music has been labelled abstract and aleatoric.

Aleatoric music is music that contains the random element of chance. The composer gives his performers 'choices of muisc', and as a result no two performances are the same. In the work *Zyklus* (Circles), for example, the performers can choose which path to follow in the piece – left to right, up or down, zig-zag – there are many options. He has also composed pieces to be performed live with an electronic tape, such as *Kontakte*, and has been crucial to the development of graphic notation.

Perhaps his most innovative idea has been to try and release performers from the shackles of gravity, and he started to experiment with the idea of flying his musicians through the air. This idea reached full growth with the piece *Helikopter – Streichquartett* in 1996, wherein four string players are located in helicopters. The piece is played with each of the players in a different helicopter with a click track to keep them together. The sound of their instruments, mixed with the sound of the helicopters, is transmitted to the audience in the concert hall below through loudspeakers.

Stockhausen's music, although extremely controversial, has been very influential. Prominent and important figures in the world of rock, rap and hip-hop have paid him tributes galore. Without him, the world of sampling and techno might not have developed to such an extent.

Stimmung

Six vocalists and six microphones (soprano 1 & 2, alto, tenor 1 & 2/baritone, bass)

This work was written in 1968 following a commission from the city of Cologne for the Collegium Vocale – a choir specialising mainly in the works of the composer J. S. Bach. The piece was inspired after the composer and his family visited Madison, Connecticut, USA in March of that year. The work contains many elements:

- the main inspiration was visiting Mexico, and walking through the ancient tribal ruins in *Oaxaca, Merida*, and *Chichenitza*. In Stockhausen's own words, "I became a *Maya*, a *Toltec*, or a *Zatopec*," i.e. the ancient Aztec gods. Stockhausen used these magic names in Stimmung.
- two extremely erotic and graphic poems are also included – poems written by the composer himself a year previously "during amorous days"
- the third element in the work that should be mentioned is the use of everyday words like *Saturday* or *Alleluia*
- the last element is imitation of animal noises such as the screech of an owl or the lowing of a cow

In a letter to his friend Gregory Rose, director of *Singcircle* who sing the piece on the accompanying CD, Stockhausen noted the following:

"I began humming, did not sing loudly anymore, settled on the low B flat, started again and wrote Stimmung, trying out everything myself by humming the overtone melodies. Nothing oriental, nothing philosophical: just the two babies, a small house, silence, loneliness, night, snow, ice: a pure miracle".

Before listening:

1. *Stimmung* literally means 'tuning', but the word has two meanings:
   a) It refers to tuning in the sense of singing.
   b) It also suggests psychological tuning between one performer and another. This was essential if the work was to be performed successfully.

   The work is divided into a number of 'moments' and before the singers can progress to the next moment, they have to sense that the entire ensemble is ready to do so. This means that every performance of the work is different.

2. The musical language of the work is all based on the dominant 9th chord. This chord, with Bb as the root note from the bass, derives from the natural harmonics of the note itself. Here is a dominant 9th chord.

Harmonics: 2nd 3rd 4th 5th 7th 9th

3. The singers are given a formal plan, pages of magic names of the gods, syllabic models where the soloists receive directions on how to intone and a page of poetry. They can use these in whatever order they want.

In the extract on the accompanying CD, it should be remembered that this is one interpretation by *Singcircle* directed by Gregory Rose. Another performance could be in a totally different order. That is what makes the work aleatoric.

LISTEN FOR:

- the word *alleluia* from the alto on D while the other voices chant
- the chanting on the vowels 'u' and 'i' by the lower voices, and the word *phoenix* sung clearly by the tenor on Bb
- alto and soprano 2 joining the chanting and voicing the word *phoenix* on Ab
- the 'magic name' *USI-NENO* (the sun god of Timor, Indonesia), voicing without pitch by the tenor
- the remaining voices taking their cue from the magic name and everyone chanting *USI-NENO* in unison and then in minor 7ths. The chord is fuller here
- the chord diminishing into unison as everyone chants on Ab. The word *kommit* is heard (like the screech of a barn owl) repeatedly from the soprano. The texture here is thin, with just two left singing at one stage.
- the bass entry is heard on the bottom Bb note, tenor 2 on F and tenor 1 on a higher Bb chanting meaningless words.
- the above is in quintuplet rhythms (*mundaogwro* and *mukomugwro*) while *moo* (like a cow) and *guru* (like a dove) are voiced.
- finally the voices are all heard in downward glissandi before the baritone chants *AHURA-MAZDA* – the Persian god of wisdom.

FURTHER LISTENING:
Stockhausen: *Gruppen*
Ligeti: *Lux Aeterna*

HENRYK GÓRECKI
b.1933 (Poland)

'I was born in Silesia… the ancient land of Poland…. but three cultures have lived there alongside each other: Polish, Czech and German… No-one can choose the time and place of their birth………'
(Henryk Mikołaj Górecki. Zakopane, Poland, July 1997)

It is not surprising therefore that Górecki's music is so diverse, displaying a wide range of different styles. The influence of serialism can be seen on his early pieces, in the Second Viennese School tradition. His Polish Catholicism is evident in a number of works such as his choral pieces. His *Old Polish Music* (1967-9) as well as one 'song' or movement from the Third Symphony (*Symphony of Sorrowful Songs*) are based on folk music. Some of his more recent music from the 1970s and 1980s has been called 'holy minimalism' and some producers in the rock music scene have remixed and re-released some of his more recent compositions.

Following his early education in Poland, Górecki went on to Paris to study. There he encountered the works of Webern, Messiaen and Stockhausen, which had been banned in Poland by the government of the day. He became Professor of Music at the University of Katowice in 1975, but he resigned in protest against the government's decision not to allow Pope John Paul II to visit the city.

His music has a strong emotional quality as well as a clarity of sound, a combination that has ensured his popularity as a classical composer. After the fall of communism in Poland in 1989, he came more and more to public attention. Indeed, the 1993 CD of his Third Symphony sold not only more copies than any other classical piece ever, but also more than the best selling rock stars heading the pop charts at the time.

Totus Tuus
Mixed chorus a cappella

This work was first performed by the Catholic Warsaw Theological Academy during Pope John Paul II's visit to the city in 1987 and was dedicated to him. This work comes from the more recent period in Gorecki's life. From his time in Katowice onwards his compositions have been much more tonal than his earlier more avant-garde pieces.

Many features of his more recent works appear in this work, such as:
- the use of tonal, diatonic chords in conjunct motion with one note at a time changing in the chord progression
- the occasional 7th chord, although he often uses 7ths and 4ths as suspensions or in passing chords
- much repetition
- modulation to distant and unexpected keys, suggesting that the work belongs to the twentieth century rather than an earlier period
- the homophonic texture of the whole piece
- a constant pulse

The words, which are very simple, come from a poem by Maria Boguslawska, wife of the Polish composer Witold Lutoslawski,:

Maria!	Mary!
Totus tuus sum, Maria,	I am completely yours, Mary,
Mater nostri Redemptoris.	Mother of our Redeemer.
Virgo Dei, virgo pia	Virgin Mother of God, blessed virgin,
Mater mundi Salvatoris	Mother of the world's Saviour.
Totus tuus sum, Maria	I am completely yours, Mary!

Much of the scoring is for SSATTB, although Gorecki does not constantly use six voices throughout the piece. He is able to vary the texture of the voices as needed, usually to fit the meaning of the words. It is an ideal work for studying harmony and chord analysis.

LISTEN FOR:

Maria! *(Lento assai. Molto esspressivo)*

• two equal phrases being repeated with the full choir singing *ff* in a homophonic style. The chords move from Ab major triads in the root position to a dissonant chord and back again through an auxilliary note (D) in the second soprano and second tenor. The phrases end on a Bb major chord in its second inversion

Totus tuus sum, Maria. *(Lo stesso tempo ma tranquillo e dolce cantabile)*

• a contrasting phrase which matches the words, with a more introvert and meditative style. The texture is decreased to four voices, and the key of the music, Eb major, becomes evident. The bass voices move down step by step and come to rest on an Eb chord in its last inversion. The dynamics also respond to the change in mood – *p*.

Mater nostri Redemptoris

• the four voices singing, beginning with a minor 7th chord and the soprano and bass moving in contrary motion and coming to rest on an Eb chord, once again in its last inversion

Virgo Dei, virgo pia

• the same material as *Totus tuus sum*, Maria, only that the phrase now ends on an unexpected cadence on the relative submediant C minor chord

Mater mundi Salvatoris

• a small change in the chords once again, a minor 7th chord opening the phrase and the soprano and bass moving in contrary motion. The words *mater mundi* are sung three times, with an auxiliary note in the third statement, followed by slightly more dissonant chords on the word *Salvatoris*.

• A G pedal note is also used on this word, and the last chord is the tonic in its first inversion.

Totus tuus sum, Maria

• the previous material returns, but now the Eb triad broadens into an augmented triad, and the section ends with a brief C minor passage (relative submediant), followed by a dominant 9th chord which leads on to a new section on the words *Maria!*

The new section begins with a beautiful and unexpected modulation to E major and C# minor, using the bass as a pivot note. From this point until the end of the excerpt, the style remains similar and a loop from the last word of the poem (*Maria!*) leads the words and music back once again to the opening material. A series of enharmonics brings about the modulations.

LISTEN FOR:

• an engaging enharmonic on the C#/Db note on the middle syllable Mar-i-a with the new section opening in Ab major

• another enharmonic on the Ab/G# note, bringing the tonality back to E major/C# minor

• the dominant chord in C# minor (G# major) becomes a sub-dominant chord in Eb major (Ab), and the material again returns to the opening chords

FURTHER LISTENING:
Gorecki: *Symphony No. 3*
Pärt: *Cantus in Memoriam Benjamin Britten*

STEVE REICH
b.1934 (USA)

Steve Reich is one of the great innovators in the world of taped music and American minimalism. He initially studied philosophy, but turned to composition in his late twenties, studying with Berio and Milhaud in the 1960s.

His music is characterized by a strong regular beat, diatonic and tonal harmony, and he is associated with composers such as Phillip Glass and, more recently, John Adams. His music is deeply rooted in recent American musical traditions, with repetitive motifs or melodic figures similar to riffs in rock 'n' roll music, or be-bop in jazz. However, in common with other minimalist composers, Reich's music also includes many new European techniques that have an academic tendency, first seen in the work of composers like Stockhausen. A prominent feature of his work is the use of electronic equipment.

Different Trains –
1st Movement
'America – Before the war'

String quartet and pre-recorded tape

The directions for performing this work are noted in great detail at the beginning of the score. The piece *Different Trains* is for a live string quartet and a recorded tape. The tape features music by three other string quartets and samples of spoken words. In the performance hall, the quartet is amplified, and plays along with the prepared tape. The two sound elements have to be played through a pair of loudspeakers; the live instruments through one and the tape through the other. In the words of the composer, "there should be no doubt which is which."

The work is based on the composer's memories as a young boy, when his mother and father were separated and he had to travel between Los Angeles and New York. He recorded certain characters from his childhood such as his governess, Virginia Mitchell and an old train porter, Lawrence Davis. The voices on the tape describe their memories of train journeys long ago, before the war. As his family also has Jewish connections, he recorded the memories of people who had lived through the Holocaust. He selected samples of their voices and imitated them, using the instruments to play the notes and rhythms closest to their speech inflexion. He also included real train noises from the steam age.

In minimalist music, listen in particlular for slight changes in the music every now and then. It may be a small change of note – a tone up or down - an addition to a motif, or a subtle change of rhythm. The final effect is exciting and interesting.

the opening... (string quartet) ♩ = 94.2

LISTEN FOR:

- the repetitive, continual ostinato from the string quartet imitating the rhythm of a train on the tracks with the 4th an important interval in the ostinato
- the tonal, diatonic harmonies, characterised by the 4th and 7th intervals
- the strong, regular rhythm, with the tempo mark strictly observed
- the small changes that occur, e.g. the appearance of an additional cello, so that the music slowly increases in dynamics until it reaches the high-pitched sound of the train's horn for the first time, imitated by 2nd violin and viola
- the sound of the train changing its 'note' – sometimes by just a semitone
- the dynamics fading in preparation for the next section

'from Chicago to New York' .... (voice of Virginia Mitchell) ♩=108

(from Chi-ca-go to New Yo-rk)

LISTEN FOR:

- the quieter dynamics in order to hear Virginia's voice
- the key change from F major to D♭ major to match the inflexion of the voice
- the major 7th chords in the harmony
- the string quartets introducing the new rhythms for four bars to prepare for the spoken words. The time signature changes from 2/4 to 3/8 every other bar for the same reason
- the appearance of a cello, creating the slightest change in texture
- the dialogue between speech and instruments
- the occasional subtle change in the order of the speech sample

'one of the fastest trains'...........(Virginia Mitchell) ♩ = 97

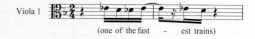

(one of the fast - est trains)

LISTEN FOR:

- the new rhythms, again to match the speech before it is heard
- the key change to match the new harmonies in the sentence
- the sound of the steam train concording with the music!
- the speech motif repeated by the viola, but not regularly – another subtle change

'the crack train from New York' ....(Lawrence Davis) ♩= 84

(the crack train from New York)

LISTEN FOR:

- the sounds of the trains in 4ths sometimes changing to 5ths
- the cello imitating the voice this time because it is lower-pitched
- the same continual rhythm from the strings
- words repeated within the phrase at times, the instruments repeating at other times

'from New York to Los Angeles'... (Lawrence Davis) ♩= 69

(from New York to Los An - ge - les)

LISTEN FOR:

- the return of the viola to imitate the voice
- the sounds of trains in 4ths, sometimes 5ths but on different notes from the previous section
- another key
- some words repeated almost in 'rap' style

FURTHER LISTENING:
Reich: *Variations for Orchestra*
Adams: *Short Ride in a Fast Machine*

OTHERS

71

KARL JENKINS
b.1944 (Wales)

As a composer, he recognises no boundaries - musical, commercial, geographical or cultural. His is a way of thinking and composing that is perfectly in tune with the spirit of the times.

The above quotation appeared in the Classic FM magazine and is a fitting description of the composer from Wales who has become known the world over. Karl Jenkins, the composer of the best-selling album *Adiemus, Song of Sanctuary* was born in Penclawdd near Swansea, and started his diverse career as an oboe player in the National Children's Orchestra. He studied in the Cardiff University and the Royal Academy of Music in London, and spent most of the subsequent years as a jazz player in the famous Ronnie Scott Club in Soho, London. He has composed for television, and his music has been used in several well known commercials. He won an award for the music which appeared in the *De Beers* diamonds commercial and the composer went on to compose *Palladio*, using the commercial's theme as the first movement.

His first breakthrough came with the *Adiemus* project in the mid 1990s. His first album, *Song of Sanctuary* was followed by another four. Other works which have won acclaim in recent years are *The Armed Man: A Mass for Peace* (1999) and his *Requiem* (2005).

Zarabanda or Sarabande

This is a dance originating in fifteenth century Spain which became well known after becoming a favourite in the classical guitar repertoire. It became part of the Baroque suite in the seventeenth and eighteenth centuries. It is a slow dance in triple time with the accent on the second beat, as seen in the opening bars.

When he was composing *Dances of Time*, Jenkins was invited by UNESCO to perform *Adiemus* in Palma, Mallorca. He composed this piece specially for that occasion. The text here makes exclusive use of the letters in UNESCO, in various permutations. The work was performed in Palma in March 1998.

Zarabanda from Adiemus III: Dances of Time

Voices and orchestra with an expanded percussion section

To Karl Jenkins, *Adiemus* was more of an extended project than a composition, and many features can be heard which are common to the five albums:

- every album is a collection of short pieces. Each one also has its own central theme, with the rest of the piece revolving around that theme
- in general, all pieces include a melody in close harmony, against an orchestral background
- the pieces do not include words as such; instead the singers sing words created by the composer himself and which do not belong to any known language. The 'language' of Adiemus has been structured carefully so that the words do not attract too much attention. The majority of those words end in a vowel. The voices, therefore, are treated more or less as any other instrument.
- the musical language of *Adiemus* has been influenced by classical music as well as world music. Its tonality is conventional most of the time and the harmonies display the influence of gospel and African music (parallell chords). The occasional suspension enhances the harmony, also the occasional false relation, suggesting jazz influences
- what is more typical in the musical language, the element that gives Karl Jenkins's music that unique flavour, is his unpredictable chord sequences and his modulations to distant keys.
- the rhythms in Adiemus III are fairly conventional but the time signature which the composer use are often more adventurous. The percussion section, when heard extensively, gives the music a primitive feel
- in *Zarabanda,* the word *tribal* above some of the vocal sections, instruct the singers to produce a more open sound. Jenkins chose Miriam Stockley for the recordings because of the quality of her voice and she was accompanied on *Adiemus III* by the Adiemus Singers from Finland
- *Adiemus III: Dances of Time* includes several dances such as the Pavanne, Ländler, Sarabande, Waltz and Minuet, all of which are part of the classical repertoire. Others such as the Rhumba and Tango are Latin-American.

The piece is divided into sections, with slight variations in the words.

LISTEN FOR:

Seno suno

- The double basses and celli playing low pedal notes with typical Sarabande rhythms –sounding almost like a drone

- the percussion instruments play polyrhythms – the more prominent ones are by the *rek* (an Arabic tambourine),the *cabasa* and the *tabla* (an Indian tabla-baya, which is a pair of drums, one wooden drum and the other made of metal)

- the sweet melody by the treble recorder
- the pedal notes also by the voices singing *seno suno*

Suno senuso, Sono secuno and Cococo cococoso

- the melody by the voice singing the Sarabande

- the entry of the strings softening the texture and the suspensions by the horn a few bars later
- *sono secuno* – the words being developed slightly
- the rising sequences leading up to a small codetta - *cococo*
- the unexpected chord sequences
- the instrumental interlude at the end of the section when the recorder is heard playing the *suno senuso* theme, leading up the the start of the next section

Suno Secuno - cose nocus

- the timbre of the voices developing a harder quality – the word 'tribal' appears in the score
- the wind instruments play syncopated triplets

- a fuller texture and louder dynamics
- the increasingly chromatic chord sequences, and some imitation and free counterpoint in the voices
- the dramatic silent beats before the next section

Seno Suno

- the opening section returning and the recorder appearing once again
- the last chord of the previous section, G major, creating a striking false relation with the quiet E major chord in this section
- harmonics by the violin – listen carefully!

Conucono nono cu

- the dramatic change in dynamics – the brass section includes three trumpets, four trombones and six french horns
- the timpani emphasising the rhythms of the Sarabande with a tonic pedal note
- the voices singing the opening section, heard a few bars earlier by the recorder
- the voice sections being repeated over a different chord sequence which include the dominant 7th and minor 7th
- the piece closes with the word *Cu* – the instruments and voices play and sing an unusually long note and the percussion section sustains the rhythm, culminating in a rousing finale

In addition to the orchestral instruments, Jenkins includes an extended percussion section in *Dances of Time*. In this piece, you can hear the following:

triangle	chekere	rek	doholla
cabasa	timpani	cow bell	tom-toms
tablas	guiro	cymbal	

FURTHER LISTENING:

Karl Jenkins: *Requiem*
Richard Rodney Bennett: *Murder on the Orient Express*

GEORGE BENJAMIN
b.1960 (England)

George Benjamin was born in London and first came to prominence as a composer and pianist on Radio 3 when he was only thirteen years old. At sixteen he was accepted as one of Oliver Messiaen's pupils (the youngest in the class) at the Paris Conservatoire, where he also studied the piano with the composer's wife, Yvonne Loriod. He then returned to the UK to study at King's College, Cambridge with Alexander Goehr. His work *Ringed by the Flat Horizon* was performed at the Proms in London while he was still a 20-year-old student – the youngest composer ever to have his work performed at the Proms. He later taught composition at the Royal College of Music and is currently a Professor of Composition at King's College, London.

Since the 1980s, he has worked frequently at IRCAM (*Institut de Recherche et Coordination Acoustique/Musique*) which is associated with the Pompidou Centre in Paris. From its inception by Pierre Boulez, the Centre has been the birthplace of the latest and most innovative concepts in electronic music. It has become a focus point for composers who from time to time are invited to the centre to experiment.

In general terms, Benjamin's music is still within the classical tradition because of his adherence to motifs and forms, but the techniques are new. He has combined various technical resources for sampling and recording with live music, in particular with the 4X – an IRCAM computer.

Antara
2 flutes, 2 synthesizers and ensemble

This piece was composed in 1985-7 when Benjamin was invited to IRCAM. *Antara* is the Peruvian word for panpipes. When Benjamin walked up from the underground IRCAM studios during his research work in 1984, a group of Peruvian buskers were playing outside. In Benjamin's words: "it was striking to see that huge, metallic building *(The Pompidou Centre)* completely dominated by the sound of those little bamboo tubes."

Antara's Instrumentation:
- 2 flutes (doubling as 2 piccolos)
- 2 Yamaha KX88 synthesizers connected to the 4X computer (representing the sound of the panpipes)
- ensemble:
  2 trombones (doubling as 2 bass trombones)
  2 percussion players playing (amongst other things) bells, drums and metal anvils
  3 violins, 2 violas, 2 cellos, double bass

Both synthesizers play four kinds of different panpipe sounds.
i)   'solo' – homophonic, virtuoso
ii) 'nat' – panpipe chords, over a range of several octaves, and able to play wide glissandi
iii) 'breath' – an 'aeolian' sound (more ancient), sampled from panpipes without the embouchure mouthpiece
iv) 'pizz' – with a quick 'push' in the sound, very staccato, and able to play very fast tremoli

As you can see in the plan on the next page, four loudspeakers are part of the ensemble. The 'solo' is heard through the two front speakers, the 'nat' and 'breath' from all four, and the 'pizz' from the two back speakers, which are more powerful.

Benjamin provides detailed instructions in the music to include micro-tones - intervals of less than one semitone. In order to do this, he has devised new notation:

$\text{d} = {}^{1}/_{4}$ tone flat $\ddagger = {}^{1}/_{4}$ tone sharp $\#\# = {}^{3}/_{4}$ tone sharp

$\uparrow = + {}^{1}/_{8}$ tone $\downarrow = - {}^{1}/_{8}$ tone

$\Uparrow = + {}^{1}/_{16}$ tone $\Downarrow = - {}^{1}/_{16}$ tone

In addition, he provides a detailed seating plan for the performers.

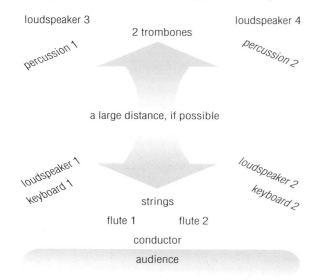

Before you listen:

Despite all the unconventional material and techniques, the structure of the work is to some extent 'classical', although this may be unintentional. The piece contains clear elements of the sonata form.

Exposition	Development	Recapitulation	CODA

The wind intruments have two main themes, following the first and second subject idea from the sonata form. They are constantly repeated and developed.

FURTHER LISTENING:
George Benjamin: *Viola, Viola*
Thomas Adès: *Asyla*

Exposition Section.

LISTEN FOR:

- the opening melody by the panpipe, which could be labelled **1st subject** (or main theme). This is the 'solo' sound and detailed instructions are provided in the score referring to the dynamics,

- the '**2nd subject**' following immediately, developing from what Benjamin calls a 'hocketing melody' – a motif which is repeated as if it is dancing from one flute to another, with the strings appearing in the background

- a development of the above motifs with the strings employing a variety of styles and techniques - pizzicato and tremoli. They are also instructed to play near the bridge (sul pont) or on the fingerboard (sul tasto). The occasional harmonic by the double bass also creates interest in the texture

- a very contrapuntal texture, with the main themes being stretched and developed constantly

- drum rolls

- ostinato by the cellos, often in a rocking rhythm before the appearance of the panpipe

- instruments playing at the extremes of their range and dynamics, often reaching unusually high or low notes after a glissando

- a growling sound by the trombone (ff feroce) and a loud sound by the metal anvils, denoting the end of the Exposition, since the two main subjects are then plainly developed

GLOSSARY

a capella – unaccompanied.

accelerando – to increase speed; abbreviated to *accel.*

acciacatura – a crushed note linked to a note of a certain duration.

absolute music – instrumental music that exists for its own sake.

alberti bass – broken chords which form an accompaniment to a melody; a series of chords treated as arpeggios.

aleatoric – music which depends on chance.

allargando – becoming slower and 'broader', often with an accompanying crescendo.

antiphony – music which is performed by two semi-independent choirs or groups of instruments interacting with one another, often singing alternate musical phrases ("call and response").

appogiatura – a dissonant note - usually a step above or below- that 'leans' on a harmony note, taking part of its time value.

arco – playing with the bow, as opposed to *pizzicato* in string music.

aria – a self-contained song for solo voice, usually part of an opera.

arpeggio - chord where the notes are played or sung in succession rather than simultaneously. The word comes from the Italian for "in the manner of the harp."

atonality – the opposite of tonality; no adherence to any system of key or mode.

augmented interval – a major or perfect interval increased by a semitone.

auxilliary note – a passing note which, instead of proceeding to another note, returns to the one it has just left.

bagpipes – wind instrument with a reedpipe and finger holes (chanter) inserted into a bag.

bitonality – the use of two different keys at the same time. Stravinsky's *Rite of Spring* is often credited with popularising bitonality.

bluegrass – a form of American roots music, popular in the South East of the USA, with its own roots in English, Irish and Scottish traditional music. as well as rural African-American music, jazz, and blues.

broken chords – playing a chord as individual notes rather than simultaneously, usually in accompaniment.

cadence – melodic or harmonic motion usually at the end of a phrase, section or movement.

cadenza – a decorated or embellished section, usually towards the end of a solo concerto (sometimes improvised).

canon – a device in counterpoint where a melody in one voice or part is imitated note by note by other voices or instruments, often overlapping the original.

ceilidh – an evening of Scottish / Irish music and dance.

chamber music – music for a small orchestra, consisting typically of pairs of oboes, bassoons and horns, and a small number of strings. Flutes, clarinets, trumpets and timpani are added as required.

chanting – simple melody, usually unaccompanied, for singing unmetrical texts.

chord(al) sequence - a series of chords.

chromatic – the use of sharps and flats; music containing many notes from outside the given key.

classical diminution – a melodic device where the time values of the melody notes are shortened, e.g. a melody moving in minims and crotchets would change to crotchets and quavers.

close harmony – where notes of the chords are all fairly closely spaced, not extending beyond the interval of about a 12th.

cluster chords – a group of notes that are placed very close together to form a chord.

coda – an addition, played after the main structure of a piece or melody has ended.

codetta – a short coda: a passage added to the end of a composition to give a greater sense of finality.

concertino - the smaller group of instruments in a concerto grosso.

concerto – a piece for one soloist (solo concerto) or more than one (concerto grosso) and orchestra.

concerto grosso – a composition in which a group of solo instruments is heard in alternation with the strings or with the orchestra as a whole.

contrapuntal – music containing counterpoint.

contrary motion –when two 'voices' or 'parts' diverge and move in different directions.

countermelody - a sequence of notes to be played simultaneously with a more prominent melody. It is usually in a subordinate role, and is heard in a texture consisting of a melody plus accompaniment.

counterpoint – the combination of more than one distinct melodic lines, often independent in contour and rhythm.

diatonic – the exclusive use of notes belonging to one key in the major-minor tonal system.

diminished interval – a major or perfect interval decreased by a semitone.

discordant – dissonant chord or interval.

dissonance – a clash between adjacent notes of the scale, creating the expectation of a resolution.

da capo – repeat from the beginning (D.C.)

dodecaphony – note-row, a method of composition where all 12 notes of octave are employed, and all treated on an equal footing (no tonic, dominant, sub-dominant notes etc.).

dominant – the 5th degree of the major or minor scale.

drone – a steady or constantly reiterated note or notes, usually on the keynote or dominant.

dynamic – varying degrees of loudness and softness.

ensemble – a group of singers or instrumentalists of any size, often applies to a chamber music group.

enharmonics - a note (or key signature) which is the equivalent of some other note, C# and Db.

entry - the audible appearance of a melody or motif/subject distinctly heard in one or more instruments or voices, usually in contrapuntal music.

episode – a section of music heard between main subject entries in fugal writing or between main themes, e.g. in rondo or ritornello forms.

false relation – simultaneous appearance in different voices of two modally conflicting notes with the same letter name, often the major and minor 3rds of the same triad.

fanfare – a flourish of brass instruments, usually trumpets, often for ceremonial purposes.

finale – the last movement of a symphony, concerto or sonata or the closing act of an opera.

fingerboard (in string instruments) – strip of hardwood glued to the neck of a stringed instrument, where the strings are stopped with the fingers.

fugue – a composition where three or more voices enter one after another, as if 'chasing' the preceeding voice; the first voice is known as the 'subject'; the second is the 'answer', transposing to the dominant; the third enters with the original subject.

gamelan – a term for instrumental ensembles in Indonesia and Malaysia, consisting mainly of percussion instruments.

glissando – a sliding movement from one note to another.

harmonic (in string instruments) – touching the string very lightly at its centre or a third of its length, inhibiting the formation of the basic note, but creating an octave or an octave plus a 5th higher.

hemiola – when two bars in triple metre are performed as if they were notated as three bars in duple metre or vice versa.

homophonic – music where one voice or part is melodic and the others mainly chordal and acting as accompaniment.

imitation – the repetition of a motif or idea in other voices.

improvisatory – to compose, play or sing on the spur of the moment; prominent in jazz and folk music in particular.

instrumental interlude – played between sections of a vocal work, e.g. between acts in operas.

interval – the distance in pitch between two notes, e.g., C – D above is a 2nd; C – A (below) is a 3rd.

inversion – turning a chord, interval, counterpoint or theme upside down. A chord is inverted when it is not in its *root position*.

juxtaposition – side by side.

melisma – a section of a song in which one syllable flowers out into a passage of several notes; sometimes called a 'slur'.

minimalism – work which is stripped down to its most fundamental features and which often involves repetition.

minuet and trio – originally a stately dance in triple metre and in ternary form often used in the Baroque suite and Classical symphony, sonata and string quartet.

modal scale – scales based on modes (see *modes, page 79*).

modulation – changing key.

monodic – solo song / instrumental piece or unison chant; one line of texture.

monotonic – single, unvaried tone.

motif – a melodic, rhythmic musical unit which brings unity to a composition; often repeated during the piece.

mute – a device for muffling the sound of an instrument; placed on the bridge of a string instrument or into the bell of a brass instrument.

non div – an instruction to pairs of instrument not to divide the written two notes between them, but to play them both (usually in string writing).

obligato – prominent instrumental countermelodies, e.g., an orchestral instrument with a semi-solo role accompanying a voice.

orchestration – the art of combining instruments when composing for the orchestra, or scoring an existing work for orchestra.

ostinato – a fairly short melodic, rhythmic or chordal phrase repeated continuously throughout a piece or section.

parallel chords – chords moving in parallel motion.

pedal note – one long sustaining note or a repetition of one note, usually (but not necessarily) in the bass register.

penillion – Welsh word for 'verses'; 'penillion singing' is the traditional art of singing poetry to harp accompaniment.

pentatonic – a scale of five notes.

pivot note – a note belonging to more than one chord or key, often used to modulate.

pizzicato – plucked rather than bowed (for string instruments).

polyphonic – music in two or more parts, with each part being rhythmically or melodically independent (see counterpoint).

polyrhythms – use of different rhythms at the same time in separate parts of the music.

polytonality – the use of more than one key at the same time.

prelude – an introduction to something further; a genre of music for solo instruments, mainly the piano, often in improvisatory style.

programatic music – music expressing mood, a narrative or a pictorial image, the opposite of 'absolute music'.

quarter tone – an interval half as wide as a semitone.

quintuplets – five notes, to be performed in the time of four, indicated by the figure 5 placed above or below.

raga – a Hindu scale which includes quarter tones and even smaller intervals.

thala – a rhythmic pattern or series of notes, usually associated with Indian music.

range – the set of notes that is possible for any instrument (or voice) to play or sing.

recitative – solo singing which sounds like the spoken word, free in rhythm with very little structured melody; sometimes imitated in instrumental music.

rhapsody – an instrumental piece in one movement, often based on popular, national or folk melodies, often having an improvisatory element.

ripieno – a passage of music played by the whole orchestra rather than a solo performer or a group of solo performers (similar to 'tutti').

rondo form – a form used in the Classical period where the main melody returns between sections of music called 'episodes' (A-B-A-C-A-D-A etc.).

root position (in a triad) – the root of a chord is the note from which it takes its name, e.g. the G major chord has G as its root.

scherzo – a bright and lively passage of music, sometimes an independent piece but originally a movement in a sonata or symphony.

semitone – the smallest interval used in Western music, e.g. from B to C or from C to C#.

scotch snap – a short note, on the beat, followed by a long one, occupying the rest of the beat.

sequences – the repetition of a melody at another level, higher or lower.

serialism – see chapter on Webern.

sonata – a composition for solo instrument (with accompaniment if needed) in three movements- fast-slow-fast.

sonata form – the typical form of one movement of a sonata, usually the first (and not the form of a whole sonata) consisting of two main themes and in three sections, Exposition, Development and Recapitulation.

stretto – a fugal device where entries follow closely in succession, each entry overlapping the next.

subdominant – the fourth degree of the major or minor scale. The 'sub' refers to the position of the subdominant a 5th below the tonic, whereas the dominant is a 5th above.

superimposition – a compositional technique where one melody or motif is placed and played simultaneously with another.

suspension – a form of discord when a note in one chord is held over as a momentary part of the chord which follows, resolving by falling a degree to a note which is part of the second chord.

symphonic poem – a piece of music, usually in one movement, which includes literary, dramatic and pictorial elements.

syncopation – the displacement of the normal musical accent from a strong beat to a weak one; important in jazz, ragtime and other popular music cultures.

texture (thick, thin etc) – describes the vertical build of the music – the relationship between its parts.

tierce de picardie – a major 3rd in a tonic chord at the end of a piece which is otherwise in a minor key, changing the expected minor chord into a major one.

timbre – the very essence of a sound; the characteristics that differentiates one instrumental sound or voice from another.

toccata – a piece in a free and idiomatic style, traditionally for the keyboard, often containing virtuoso elements.

tone poem – see symphonic poem.

tonal – an adherence to a certain key or mode.

tonal centre - a pull towards one note, usually pivotal, rather than a set of notes which form a scale or a key.

tonality – a term to describe the harmonic language of a piece of music.

tonic – the 1st degree of the major or minor scale.

tremolo/i – the fast repetition of a note or chord.

triad – a chord of three notes, usually a 'root' with the 3rd and 5th above it.

tritone – an interval of three whole tones, i.e. the augmented 4th (C – F#) or diminished 5th (C – Gb).

tutti – whole orchestra.

vaudeville – a kind of variety show, popular in America from the 1880s onwards.

whole-tone scale – a scale of six whole tones (intervals of two semitones).

whole tone scale

MODES AND THEIR MODULATIONS

cwmni cyhoeddi GWYNN